LEANING INTO LIFE

James Vander Kamp

James Vander Kamp

DEDICATION

This book is for those I love beginning with my wife Elaine and extending to our children, grandchildren, our siblings and extended family. Without them I don't know where I would be. It is also for a special group of people, my writers' club: Hans Benes, Lynn Haass, Pat Karam and Mimi Normile. Without them, this book would never have seen the light of day. My thanks and appreciation to all.

James Vander Kamp

CONTENTS

A Brief Prolegomena
The Train

1. The Epic Journey
2. The Power of Family
3. Putting the Horse before the Cart
4. School Days and Beyond
5. The Family Car
6. Memories of My Dad
7. Turning Points (1)
8. Transitions
9. Turning Points (2)
10. Baseball Been Berry Good to Me
11. On Learning to Work
12. Obstacles in My Early Career
13. Our One and Only Son
14. My Love Affair with Performing
15. Katydid, Our Eldest Daughter
16. The Natural Word: God's Creation
17. An Ode to Trees
18. Melissa Joy, as in Joyful
19. A letter to Mom
20. Memorable Characters
21. Andrea, Our Shining Star
22. Life Highlights: Experience is King
23. Turning Points (3)
24. Catalonia Riviera Maya
25. The Sensual and the Spiritual
26. Working Out
27. The Trip Beyond Beautiful

28. The Next Generation
29. Life Rising
30. Changing of the Guard
31. The Roadmap of My Life
32. Rhythms
33. Greenwich Lullaby
34. Adages to Live by
35. But What of Tomorrow?
36. Address to Timothy Christian High School
    Graduation, 2011

Acknowledgements

James Vander Kamp

A BRIEF PROLEGOMENA

My dear wife is the family memory maker for the generations. She creates traditions, rituals and memorable events for holidays, birthdays and other significant occasions. I, on the other hand, am the memory custodian. I do most of the photography, create albums, order DVDs, and maintain written records of important events. I don't want my own memories to die with me but to be available to the generations who follow. I am doing this now before my time runs out and things are lost forever.

When I am planning a trip, much of the fun is in the anticipation. I love maps, history, architecture, geography, and weather. I visualize so much before the actual travel occurs that my vicarious enjoyment in advance often carries me through what might be a disappointing reality. Like the mailman, neither rain, nor snow, nor gloominess can remove the pleasure of a trip well-planned. Reduce, maybe, but not eliminate it.

So too with my memoir. My memories remain vivid but are no doubt incomplete. The joy in remembering the good of my past surely obscures much that was unpleasant. Focusing on the negative only serves to magnify it, so why not stick with more of my ample positive memories? If healing can come from sharing something difficult, then I hope that I can embrace that as well. Regardless, the things I talk about are **my personal recollections**; they are not my brothers', my sister's, or friends', but mine alone.

The great thing about a memoir is that it helps me remember who I used to be while clarifying how I got to be who I am. That also means I may use a bit of myth to serve as an extension of the truth to make the story a bit more interesting.

Lies have no place in a work like this but a small bit of fantasy can serve a useful purpose.

I suppose the point of all this is to give my descendants a context for their own lives. Where we come from, both geographically and genetically, matters. Where I lived helped shape me; who I came from shaped me even more. These were all anchors to my life. I am thankful for more good memories than bad, more good people who helped form me than those who discouraged me, more positive direction on a good path than an unstructured passive approach leaving me to my own devices.

I hope my words convey so much more than episodes and anecdotes but reveal the true heart of my life.

James Vander Kamp

THE TRAIN

"It's a Beautiful Journey, so Enjoy the Ride"

At birth we boarded the train of life and met our parents. We believed they would always be traveling with us, at our side. However, at some station our parents will step off the train, leaving us on this journey alone. As time goes by, other people will board the train and they will be significant to you, like siblings, friends, the love of your life, and your children. Along the way, some will step off the train and will leave a permanent vacuum. Others will go so unnoticed that we won't even realize that they vacated their seats.

This train ride will be full of joy, sorrow, fantasy, expectations, hellos, good-byes, and farewells. To be successful on the journey means we need to have good relationships with all the passengers, requiring that we give the best of ourselves along the way.

The mystery to all aboard is that we do not know at which station we ourselves will step off. So, we must live in the best way, by loving, forgiving, and offering the best of who we are. It is important to do this because when the time comes for us to step off and leave our seat empty, we should leave behind beautiful memories for those who will continue to travel on the train of life.

I wish you a joyful journey on the train. Reap success and give lots of love. More importantly, thank God for giving you your journey. Lastly, I thank you for being one of the passengers on my train.

Anonymous

THE EPIC JOURNEY

"How did I get so old so fast and miss so much of what was going on?"

I have lived a good long time. As I write this, I am 68 years old and have experienced life in eight decades. Although my life may only have consequence for me and a few others, I thought I would try to relate my experience through the decades to what else was going on in the country and the world. So here is a whirlwind tour from my earliest memories right up to the present.

The 50s: These were my formative years, so I remember the least about them, but I can at least put them into an historical context. The country had just come out of WWII and was experiencing an unprecedented economic boom. My parents married right after the war in 1946 and were trying to establish themselves as an independent family unit. Everyone liked Ike and he served two terms as President, from 1952 – '60. I started school during this time and learned to read with Dick and Jane, I saw Spot run, and saw the house they lived in with the white picket fence. Naturally, this became the suburban ideal and our family did indeed have such a fence.

The 60s: By this decade we elected an Irish Catholic as President, JFK, an unheard-of occurrence in the history of the U.S. We also all met his family: the lovely Jackie and their two charming children, Caroline and John-John. I was maturing and graduated from high school and moved on to college. These were the hot dating years, first love, first love lost, try again. I had my first real work experiences during this time where I found out what schedules were, punching in at 5 a.m., working all the overtime I could to cover my costs for college. This was also the time when our ideals were tested as Camelot was destroyed by the assassination of the President, and just a few years later, his brother Bobby. Race wars were seething in many cities and the great peacemaker himself, Martin Luther King, was also killed. We put a man on the moon and heard that we should not ask what our country could do for us, but instead, what we could do for our country. We also learned what it was like to have a dream and that such a dream could include people of all races existing in peace.

The 70s: Real love arrived and with it, marriage! A year later, college graduation and my first professional job teaching. Despite an overwhelming win in 1972, Richard Nixon was pulled down by Watergate and resigned the presidency. Vietnam was winding down but was a hot topic on college campuses across the country. Student unrest caused lots of strife and we heard about the SDS (Students for a Democratic Society) wreaking havoc on campuses from coast to coast. This was quite a jolt for me since I was now a graduate and joining the Establishment by going to work and not marching for some higher cause. Graduation meant a move to Washington state for work and then graduate school. Within a few short years came another major move, this time to Colorado and a new job with Roundup Fellowship working with kids from broken families who had been abused and neglected. Besides the major life changes we were experiencing, the country was caught up in an oil embargo causing lines at gas stations and rising prices. Before the decade was out, we had our first two kids, a boy and a girl. After five years on the job, I became the boss (Executive Director) and was now trying to find myself at the ripe old age of 30.

The 80s: More family additions came bringing us to six in our household. This was not without significant hand-wringing however. We had already experienced the loss of both of my wife's parents earlier in the decade and found ourselves with our own "crisis pregnancy" as we approached turning 40. Add to that the need for a larger house and you can see that "circumstances were conspiring against us." Our house went up for sale and was one of five for sale **on our block!** We really saw the hand of God move as we bought a new house, sold the one we had lived in for 11 years, brought home our newest, unplanned arrival, and turned 40. Whew! Ronald Reagan took over the reins in Washington from a much-beleaguered Jimmy Carter and before the 80s were done, we saw the Berlin Wall come down and our first baby go to high school.

The 90s: This was a time of professional growth for me as we were expanding as an organization under my leadership. This was often both exhilarating and scary. We celebrated our 25th wedding anniversary and enjoyed a number of delightful family vacations which included many extended family members. This allowed our kids to know their distant cousins and laid the groundwork for their friendships today. These were the Bill Clinton years, with times that were both scandalous and economically booming. He told us "It's the economy, stupid," so why bother with a few peccadilloes? A chink in the national armor emerged as America was changing. This decade had us send our first-born off to college, teach one daughter how to drive while teaching our youngest how to ride a bike. We lost my Dad in 1997 and have lived with a heavy heart ever since. By 1998 we had our first grandchild, Christina, from our daughter Katie, so joy did come in the morning.

The 00s: The new millennium brought a big scare –Y2K – but it proved to be much ado about nothing. Shortly thereafter came the real scare: 9/11. This pushed our country into the war on terror and has created a permanent malaise world-wide. We now live in a "global community," one that exchanges goods and information with speed and precision, but one that is fraught with many fears. The internet, our friend in the previous decade, now brings us inordinate concern over our personal information being stolen or shared inappropriately. I experienced many positive gains at work and in family life as we had two college graduations, three weddings, and more grandchildren. While we were building a family legacy, our country did what had been previously unthinkable: elected a black President. Sadly, this did not prove to be an ultimate victory over racism; instead, I believe that we continue to have a significant racial divide that defies quick fixes like an election.

The 10s: As I write this, we still have a few years to go in this decade, but we have gratefully seen our fourth child get married. My mother died leaving us as the standard bearers for the Vander Kamp clan. At the moment, our grandchild tally stands at eight with a realistic possibility of more. This remains one of the greatest blessings of our life together. We traveled to Italy along the Amalfi coast and that European adventure will be forever etched in our minds. I turned 65, a retirement marker, and then retired a year later from full-time work, having spent just over 40 years at Roundup. I have had far too many physical challenges this decade, but I remain optimistic in my ability to continue to maintain a course which includes at least a modicum of physical rigor. Donald Trump prevailed as perhaps the least likely candidate to be elected in who knows how long, another indication of just how divided our country is. The coming years will be very interesting indeed. Obviously, I have stayed with my writing and, I trust, a full-blown memoir will emerge in the days ahead. I am also excited about some challenging new teaching possibilities that are emerging for me. I look forward to a future devoted to my wife and family while remaining active on a variety of fronts. Soli Deo Gloria: To God alone be the glory.

James Vander Kamp

THE POWER OF FAMILY

"Be fruitful and multiply..." Gen. 9:1

I can honestly say that family influences have dominated my life. The closeness that I experience with my wife, children and grandchildren had its roots planted in me years ago. Reflecting on my upbringing, my years at home were spent with a group that extended far beyond my nuclear family of six. I vividly recall visiting Grandma Vander Kamp at her apartment in Cicero, IL after church on Sunday mornings where coffee cake ruled supreme. I remember holidays spent with aunts, uncles and cousins, picnics in the summer with hot dogs and softball games, trips to the lake for swimming and laying on the beach, and many other family bonding experiences. Of course, we never looked at them in that way. It was just what our large extended family did. I now realize the value-added experience my parents gave me so that I could perpetuate it when our own family came along and was growing.

It is plain to me that maintaining family ties was always a priority for my Mom and Dad and that example has carried over into my life. Growing up we knew our aunts and uncles, with both of my parents having seven living siblings; our cousins, no small feat when I counted them: 18 on my mother's side and 25 on my dad's, 43 in all. Naturally, I had favorites among them, people who I was eager and glad to see when a family event was planned. Seeing Uncle Jerry or Ben always meant a livelier time than Uncle Pete or Nubs. Being with Auntie Wilma, Martha or Margaret topped time spent with Josephine or Dorothy. The lineup of highly appreciated cousins was even lengthier. This has carried over to our children and grandchildren who are not just blood relatives but good friends as well. Distance could have proven to be a fatal foe in establishing and maintaining relationships but we made it a priority to take the long trek to the upper Midwest with our children so they could see their grandparents and the rest of the family.

Even with our children grown and married, some things continue. In July 2016, we took a trip back to our old stomping grounds. We saw my younger brother John in Illinois, brother Dick in Michigan, two of Elaine's sisters, Barb and Debbie, in Holland, Michigan and ended with a swing around the lake to Wisconsin to visit my sister Pat. Most of those visits included some of their children and grandchildren as well. We talk about our lives now, but conversations always include our children and grandchildren. Our numbers are quite a bit smaller than the generation of our youth but the feelings we express are as genuine and the interest we have in each other is as keen. It remains clear that we all know what matters most.

How is it that we ended up with this perspective, this belief that blood relationships are vital for our very existence? There was no authoritarian patriarch, no overly coercive matriarch, that dictated the terms of our relationships. There was only love, that and an abiding faith that permeated everything we did and believed. We were a church-going family, but it went much deeper than that. We prayed at home, read the Bible, learned its teachings, and ultimately learned that we were part of something bigger than ourselves and our extended family. We learned that by calling ourselves Christians we were accepting Jesus as our Lord and Savior and identifying with fellow believers around the world and through the ages who shared that belief.

I am eternally grateful to my parents and extended

family for showing me the way to a much richer, more fulfilling life. It becomes increasingly clear to me that life is not about a big house, a "dream" job or a hefty income. It really comes down to matters of the heart where loving relationships rule the day and have the potential to create a lasting legacy for generations.

PUTTING THE HORSE BEFORE THE COST and Other
Tales of Growing Up

I estimate this picture was taken some time in 1951.

James Vander Kamp

As a young child in Chicago, mine was an urban existence. There were some trees on our street, even an empty lot across the street, but mostly, life was filled with houses, concrete, and blacktop. None of that really mattered though because my brother and I had two young, energetic, post-war parents who were determined to give us a better life.

In the early '50s there was a phenomenon that has long since gone away: the door to door salesman. From the iconic Fuller Brush to bars of sweet smelling soap, to the Good Humor ice cream truck, to knife-sharpening done while you wait from the push-cart, there was little need for a car or even a telephone for that matter. The world came to us and my alert mother often took advantage.

One day while playing out front with my older brother, a dazzling opportunity presented itself. Before our very eyes a pony appeared! It was led by a good-natured gent who, for a small price, could mount the local urchins and photograph them. Since we were already enamored by the painted pony, how could our mother resist? No fee was too great to pay to have her sons put aboard the dynamic steed and have their picture taken. Getting us to smile would not be a problem. (I never learned what exorbitant fee mom paid, but it was obviously worth it).

After a short few years in Chicago, our parents realized their dream and bought a house in the suburbs. Oak Park was idyllic by comparison for them to be sure. More space in a much larger home, a garage for the family car, and even an empty lot next door; what more could anyone ask for? Growing up in Oak Park was a great experience. We could freely explore up and down the street which included the aforementioned empty lot next door and an even larger space just three doors down, places where boys could play safely but never be too far from our mother's watchful eye.

As I aged we got acquainted with our neighbors. Since this was the post-war '50s, there were plenty of families on our block giving us lots of playmates. Safety was never in question; even when I was a mere 5 years old, I walked almost two blocks to kindergarten at Washington Irving School by myself. Mom never gave a thought to delivering me in person for my early education.

My brother, who was more than two years my senior, typically led the way regarding neighborhood relationships and exploits. This worked fine for a while but eventually he decided that having a younger brother tag along was not cool. That left me to develop my own set of friends starting with Eddie and Richie next door and Mark and Mary across the street. We spent hours playing "pinners" with a tennis ball on our porches in the front yard. Pinners was a simple game of throwing the ball at the front steps with your opponent standing on the lawn hoping to catch the ball wherever it went. We caught bees in jars which we proudly displayed to our parents. Summer nights brought out lightning bugs and we reluctantly let the bees go so we could allow our flashing friends to take up residence in the same jars.

It was easy to have things to do with so many similarly aged kids living on the same block. We had a mixture of younger families, older people, and even a few single women who I now assume were widows. However, we did have one particularly tense space on our block. Just a couple of doors down from where we lived was a large, old dilapidated house with an equally old lady living there, most appropriately named Mrs. Saur. We all thought the place was haunted, so we mostly stayed clear. We rarely saw her but when we did, she seemed nicer than all the appearances to the contrary. The mind of a youngster can create some rather remarkable scenarios, especially without any verifiable information to prove something one way or the other. Only age could cure those misconceptions, but by the time we were old enough to give her a chance, the house was remodeled and sold to another family. The mystery lingers, unsolved in the minds of those kids who thought the way I did.

Getting older meant expanding our borders. Bikes gave us freedom to go well beyond the safety of Cuyler Avenue. Our family was growing, so I was starting to move in the direction of my older brother, separating myself from my younger sister who I wasn't particularly interested in. She couldn't play catch, she couldn't run very fast; why would a boy want a girl around anyway? Sometimes I had to push her in her buggy down the block, so my mom could get some work done at home. This did not excite me, and it led to a few inappropriate jaunts down the sidewalk at breakneck speed. I thought that might be the only way I could tolerate my assignment.

My nonchalance and inattentiveness almost had disastrous consequences. My sister was ensconced securely within the confines of her buggy when my mother told me to gently push her back and forth to help her fall asleep. We were on our back porch and this meant I was a prisoner until she succumbed to her drowsiness. I sat down while having my hand on the handle, rolling the device with perhaps a bit more oomph than I should have. Yes, I pushed a bit too hard and the front wheels exited the platform and my sister went careening down the stairs into the yard! I quickly followed her, but she was indeed screaming as only a frightened baby could. Righting the buggy, I saw my sister crying but apparently in one piece. My mother emerged and could only imagine what I had done to not just keep Patty from sleeping but even to jeopardize her very life. There was much yelling, screaming and tears but I did escape the lash. I learned a lesson that day that I have never forgotten about how one should properly care for a younger sibling.

Since all my friends had bikes, we began to broaden our horizons in a most significant way. By the time we were 12, we headed for points both known and unknown. Yes, we could ride east, down past Austin Blvd. to the swimming pool at Columbus Park in Chicago for mid-summer refreshment, but we could also go west on Roosevelt Rd. to Miller Meadow, the Desplaines River, and other uncharted territory.

On one excursion we went into the woods and arrived at a well-hidden pond. Having ridden for about an hour, we were tired but had a keen sense of anticipation that an adventure was about to materialize. As we scanned the waterfront, we noted bulrushes, pond scum, and an occasional frog croaking, all within our sight line. Something seemed odd as I looked more closely. I blurted out for all my friends to hear, "hey, look at that log out there with all those army helmets on it. How'd they get there?" In short order, we noted a mass exodus of sun-bathing turtles take the plunge into the safety of the murky water.

Baseball was a passion for many of us but getting to see our hometown major league heroes in person seemed like a virtual impossibility. That is, of course, until I met up with Rich Smith who had an idea. His dad often took the El train downtown for work and he thought two young boys might like to do the same. His mom was equally knowledgeable, and a plan was devised. We got directions for which train to catch to Wrigley Field, where to get off and transfer, and what times we could get aboard. We had some coins in our pocket for tickets and a snack, so we were ready to roll.

James Vander Kamp

The Cubs played all their games during the day so getting back and forth on a warm summer day should keep us in daylight at all times. We walked to the El, caught the appropriate train, and off we went for a day at the ballpark. The Cubs were notoriously bad at this time, but it mattered nothing to two boys, aged 11 and 12 respectively, who finally had the chance to bask in the aura of Major League Baseball. I don't even recall the outcome of the game or who the opponent was, but I will always remember taking the train without my parents or any other adult present. We got home exhausted but happy. We had a tale to tell that far exceeded the outcome of a single ball game. We were growing up.

SCHOOL DAYS...AND BEYOND

I recognize that what I am about to say is trite, but I feel compelled to say it anyway: I really can't believe that it has been fifty years since I graduated high school. There, I said it. With that behind me, I can now make some concrete recollections regarding my school career. I remember going to Timothy Christian grade school in Cicero, Illinois. I must have started first grade in 1955 and I remember sometimes walking, sometimes taking the school bus, and sometimes taking my bike. All of this came after my successful stint in kindergarten at Washington Irving Elementary School, the only public institution I attended until graduate school.

Timothy was a place where I made friends that stayed a part of my life for the entire time I was there and even years beyond. Bosom buddy boyfriends in the early grades, first romantic interest in Junior High, high school teammates in basketball and baseball, fellow thespians in plays, and a little learning thrown in for good measure, all made for a fun and varied life. For all we might kid about not liking school or certain subjects or teachers, my school experience left many lasting positive impressions.

I lived in a mostly Dutch, church-centered community. In fact, I really didn't know many people who were outside of that circle. When I walked to school in the early years, it was with my older brother Dick. That was fine for a while, but as is so often the case, a younger sibling becomes *persona non-grata* at a point in time, causing Dick to "ditch" me and meet up with his peers apart from me. That meant that I needed to identify someone who was on my route so I could show up with a chum of my own.

James Vander Kamp

One of the first that I hooked up with was Allen Huisman, a classmate. The Huismans went to our church and his dad was my barber and they lived behind the barber shop. It was right on Roosevelt Road so it was right on my way. I palled around with Allen for several years both going to school and in other things apart from school. I also became friends with his cousin John Huisman, who became one of my best friends in grade school and high school. We were basketball teammates on the school team and softball teammates on the church team. We stayed close during college even though we attended different colleges and John was a groomsman at my wedding. After marriage, I moved far away, and we didn't stay in touch, something I regret to this day. I hope I see him at our reunion next month.

For some reason I made friends with the sons of the ministers of our church. Jerry Dykstra was the first who I remember when we were just starting school. I don't remember much about him, but we did meet up again when we were both attending Calvin College years later. His dad's successor, Rev. Hoekstra, had a son, Paul, also my age. They came when we were both fifth graders and stayed until we finished eighth grade when his dad took a call to Paterson, NJ. I also reconnected with him at Calvin when we were both trying out for the freshmen basketball team. (He made it, I didn't).

The third preacher's kid I befriended was Jonathan Bradford. Ironically, when the Hoekstra's left for New Jersey, the Bradford's were coming from there. Jonathan became a close friend during high school and beyond, serving as a second groomsman at our wedding. In fact, he and John Huisman found a car somewhere in the Chicago area that needed transport to the Northwest and they drove that car 2000 miles to our wedding.

Good friends indeed. Our friendship was rekindled years later when we both joined the same professional organization and saw each other at the annual training conference for a number of years before we both retired.

I have many good memories of kids I went to school with during my 12 years at Timothy. There were guys like Cal Van Reken, a classmate who later went on to teach at Calvin Seminary. I saw him when I attended his mother's wake about two years ago and we had a brief chat. We played a lot of basketball over the years and won a championship as seniors. His dad was our family doctor and his older sister Margie was a classmate of my brother. He also has two brothers who became doctors so they were a rather illustrious family.

Our neighborhood was full of kids in such close proximity that we always seemed to connect, whether at school, church or in related settings. Jack Schipma became a friend of mine, but our families already had a closeness that included our dads being counselors in the boys' club at our church. This expanded into us all taking an extended trip together to Niagara Falls and then to the club's convention in New Jersey in '63. Jack's mother remained close to mine until my mother died in 2016.

There were plenty of others who became friends along the way but often within a particular context. Sports teams drew us together, especially the boys on the basketball team. I suppose that stands out because we were so successful in high school, winning 56 games while losing only 11 during our last three years, including winning a championship as seniors. Those are memories I still relish and shared with fellows like Huisman and Van Reken, but also Ron Baker, John Evenhouse and Dave Schuurman. Shared experience is what pulled us together.

I also developed some real friendships with girls along the way too. The pressure associated with dating was alleviated when we performed in class plays as juniors and seniors. We were focused on a goal and that helped develop more mature ways of seeing each other, beyond the awkwardness that romance too often engenders. Ruth Oldenburger, Linda De Boer, Marcy DeVries, and Maribeth Cook were wonderful people who I came to appreciate for the skills they possessed and for the people who I really got to know on a deeper level.

[There were others who I overlooked to expedite this segment but who had an impact on my life nonetheless. Sorry that I simply couldn't include everyone].

Fifty years after graduation, our class pulled together a reunion of the class of '67. I was asked to be the M.C. for the event and I graciously accepted. The local committee put us back into the recently remodeled building from which we graduated, and we enjoyed an evening of food, reminiscing, and generally trying to become reacquainted with a large number of people who we no longer recognized. We were saved by name tags bearing our high school graduation photos so we could at least decipher who our classmates were rather than mistaking them as spouses.

We really had a wonderful time. The afore-mentioned names I listed were present in almost full force. I saw my old friend John Huisman. He was easy to spot at 6'8". He has done a number of things since college, but with the crowd beckoning, we couldn't spend too much time catching up. Thirty-two classmates out of a possible 69 survivors appeared with each of us either carrying more weight, less hair, and a heavy dose of aches, pains, and ailments. We tried not to dwell on many of those things but instead focused on professional accomplishments, children, and grandchildren. A booklet was produced which gathered pictures and fifty-year updates of people's lives, no small feat. Illustrious people of long ago were often still illustrious, but sometimes in unexpected ways. Shrinking violets showed how they had bloomed, wall flowers demonstrated that they were now off-the-wall, and potted plants exhibited vigor after they had been transplanted.

Overall, it was a most memorable time. Many conversations had to be cut short to begin one with someone else. My lasting memory was one of class cohesion, concern for one another, and simply enjoying each other's company. I heard no behind-the-back type comments, nor jealous or spiteful remarks. It was a time of remarkable harmony and genuine enjoyment of seeing those who we surprisingly missed after all these years. I was thankful to everyone who made the effort to show up and add to the flavor of a lively, remarkable night that I will not forget.

James Vander Kamp

THE FAMILY CAR

"See the USA in your Chevrolet!"

Growing up gave me many opportunities but one of the most important was how we got from here to there. As a boy in a walkable neighborhood, our primary means of transport was on foot. As we aged, bicycles got us out to even more far-flung locations. But the staple for all of us was the family car.

As a younger man, my Dad walked, took street cars or buses or, if he wanted to splurge when he was dating my Mom, took a cab. That extreme choice ended when they married and eventually bought the first car I remember, a 1951 light green Chevy. What did I know about cars? I was just a kid and knew that when we needed to go somewhere far or fast, we took the car. My Dad was uninformed regarding automobiles. He went to the gas station where the friendly guy washed your windows, checked the oil, and filled the tank. It was only when there was a deviation from that routine that Dad got flummoxed and realized how out of his league he was about maintaining his car.

When I went to college and studied sociology, I learned that we were a lower middle-class family. I didn't know that as a boy since almost everyone I knew was like us. They lived in houses like we did, had cars like ours, and had a passel of kids, usually three or more. We were happy and knew we were loved but we also knew we had places to go and people to see. That was what the car was for. We could visit our grandma, aunts and uncles and cousins who were spread around Chicago and its nearby suburban communities. Once a year we would take a vacation to Wisconsin where we lived like royalty (or so we thought) for a week.

I don't remember ever going to a store in the car except at Christmas. Our clothes all came from the Sears catalogue so there was no need to go shopping. It was only when my parents decided that I needed a suit that I was dragged to a clothier who could match my body to the right threads. That was a rare occurrence, but it did generate some excitement since most times I wore hand-me-downs from my brother, cousins, or neighbors, or got something out of the aforementioned catalogue.

Cars were mostly problematic during my growing up years. My Dad drove our only car to work six days so that meant legs or bikes got us around. If the car needed something beyond gas or oil, my Dad was stumped. That meant that different machines ended up in our garage every couple of years. From the '51 Chevy we moved on to a '53 two-tone Chevy, white roof and a black body. Pretty swanky, but not too long for our world. I remember a short-lived – months, not years - excursion in a '49 Plymouth and then a 1952 Chrysler Imperial with power windows. I thought we had really arrived with that car, but I remember my Dad being a little nervous about driving something that could be construed as out of our league. Not to worry; it had an early demise as well.

By the late '50s we had reached our full complement of children (four), so it was time to buy that highly prized middle-class commodity, a station wagon. For us that meant a yellow '55 Ford. It was roomy and had what every child longed for on a long trip: a "way back." We could climb over the back seat and have another world available to us for play or rough housing. We loved that. It served us well for several years. Of course, in short order I became too big to deposit myself back there so that space was reserved for my younger brother and sister, while my older brother and I had to share the back seat.

As I entered my teens I remember a '58 Rambler station wagon and then a move back into sedans, like the sporty, two-toned, wide-finned '59 Chevy. That was the car I got my driver's license in. Now our focus in the car changed from occasional neighborhood errands or family vacations to going on dates, if I could get the car at an opportune time. We still only had one car so competing with my Dad and brother made this a tough proposition.

By the time I was getting ready to go to college, we got a lovely '63 Chevy with a grimy blue interior. It was all-hands-on-deck when my Dad brought this beauty home one Saturday and we attacked the inside with a host of cleaning products and elbow grease. A vast improvement was made, and I was hoping my willingness to join in this project would improve my prospects of borrowing the car when needed. It helped that my brother was now in college and had a car of his own.

Within a year my brother dropped out of college and got drafted. Since my mother never got a license, I was now the heir apparent to drive her or my younger siblings where they needed to go. This also improved my dating prospects since my Dad was tired on Friday night after a hard week of work and I got use of the family car with greater frequency.

The last car I remember was a beautiful green 1968 Chevy. I had the privilege of going with my Dad as he made the rounds of dealerships to see who had the best deal. I was under the impression that we had agreed that he would go for a year-old model, not new, but by far the newest thing he had ever owned. Something must have changed somewhere along the way because he immediately began coolly dickering on a brand-new car. I was shocked, to say the least. How could he do this?

Had he secretly squirreled away a stash of Spanish doubloons or had he made off with the contents of Fort Knox while I wasn't paying attention?

I learned something that day as I watched him puff on a cigarette in a disinterested manner. Were they serious about selling this man a car or would he have to go down the street and approach a rival? I watched salesmen squirm as he told each one how their competitor had a better offer. Could they match it? Beat it? I participated in a valuable lesson that day. He sealed the deal with the last dealer who assured him no one could beat his deal. I doubt that anyone could after what I had witnessed.

He kept that car until I got married so it will stick in my memory as the last family car I rode in.

James Vander Kamp

MEMORIES OF MY DAD

"Dad. When you say his name aloud, you realize how much he means to you. Dad. His title may be short, but his influence is long and powerful."

"It's only when you grow up and step back from him – or leave him for your own home – it's only then that you can measure his greatness and fully appreciate it." Margaret Truman

When I think back over my life I realize that my Dad had a greater influence over me than I ever thought. He could be charming, funny, caring, and full of joy. He had tremendous common sense which I only came to appreciate as I attended college and then went out on my own. His lack of formal education due to a tenth-grade drop-out, in no way hindered him from achieving in the working world. A product of the Great Depression, he was born in 1921 and found out how difficult life could be when he was still a boy.

I recall him talking about going swimming in Lake

Michigan as a youth in the nude. I'm sure it was because his family didn't have money for luxuries like swim trunks. You had to be quick and sneaky if you were going to brave the frigid waters of the Lake and not be chased away by a cop who had a lakefront beat.

Times were very different then. He talked about sleeping with his two older brothers, "three in a bed," he would always say. He also talked in wistful terms about getting eleven pennies from his older brother for a day's activities. He would get up long after his brother had gone out on a job or to look for work and there would be those pennies all lined up for him to scoop into his pocket, so he could take a street car or the El train and go to the beach to swim and get a hot dog. A princely sum indeed!

One story I well recall was about when he would go out to work with his Pa on a truck at the South Water Market. This is where the produce got delivered and they might be able to load, unload or deliver fruits and vegetables if help was needed. Sometimes the goods were too damaged to send out but that meant they might be able to scavenge what was there to feed their own large family of eleven.

Sometimes, though, they struck out entirely: no work and no food to be scrounged. They would come home with nothing to show for their day out but might instead be surprised to find a bag of groceries waiting on the stoop outside their flat. It never dawned on me just how tough things were in those days because my own experience was nothing like that. We never lacked for anything that I can remember. For Dad and his family, neighbors helped neighbors because the Depression meant that virtually everyone was in a similar situation.

Getting banged up as a kid was normal then too. Though

always small, he talked about some of his play experiences as a boy, particularly playing tackle football with bigger kids and getting teeth knocked out. This, along with some very poor dental hygiene and no dental check-ups, left him with quite a few gaping holes in his mouth. Eventually, he would need a full set of dentures which always caused him to proclaim: "My teeth are like the stars; they come out every night." His dentures plagued him and there were many times when he kept them in a glass and gave us that toothless grin so that he could get some relief from wearing what must have been ill-fitting false teeth.

Despite any negatives I might have seen in my Dad's makeup, he was one of the most positive, thankful people I ever knew. He was extremely loyal to his company, Dr. Scholl's, where he started before he went off to WWII and returned to his job after his discharge from the Army. His loyalty spanned forty years of work and only ended when his company pulled up stakes in Chicago to save money on labor costs and moved to the small Southern burg of Cleveland, Tennessee. He was even asked to help with the relocation while not joining the refashioned enterprise. He never spoke ill of his company despite the hardship it caused him to lose his position and much of his pension late in life.

One of my great regrets had to do with not seeking out information on his war experience or listening during those times when he was willing to talk about where he had been, what he had seen, and what he had done. He achieved the rank of Master Sgt. and was decorated for bravery in the face of extreme fire by the Nazis while in Belgium. He received a Silver Star for that action but never talked about the circumstances under which he was decorated. In addition, he got a Purple Heart for wounds he received while fighting. As boys, my brother and I always looked at those indentations on his arm and leg, not fully understanding that he had been shot by the enemy on several occasions.

I am thankful for my Dad and do miss him. He died in 1997, but he was around long enough to know all our children and to show a positive, possessive love towards them. He became more expressive in his later years and would hug not just the grandkids but me as well. That meant a lot to me given that he showed much less affection to us growing up. For some reason a light came on that gave him permission and he could verbalize his love as well. Even the Silent Generation could be coaxed into expressing something new later in life.

James Vander Kamp

TURNING POINTS (1)

[Under this broad category I thought about identifying a variety of things that have been significant to me, even defining my life's course. I'll be naming a few of these under the **TURNING POINTS** heading but by far the most important is the one I will begin with: meeting my wife Elaine.]

"The man who finds a wife finds a treasure, and he receives favor from the Lord." Proverbs 18:22

I started college in the fall of 1967, right after I graduated high school. College was exciting but a major adjustment. From Timothy Christian High School with 300 students in Elmhurst, IL to Calvin College with 4000 in Grand Rapids, MI, I went from being a BMOC – big man on campus – to one much smaller rather nondescript student on a much larger campus. I found myself having my very own E Pluribus Unum moment, one among the many, surrounded by those who mostly seemed to be better prepared, more with it, and generally better equipped for social, academic, and athletic life than I was. I had recently broken up with a girlfriend, so I was reeling from that while I was trying to find my place on a comparatively sprawling college campus. What worked for me three months earlier might not work for me here, so my confidence was not exactly where I hoped it would be.

My freshman year brought both expected ups and downs and some unexpected: I certainly knew that college work would be harder than high school but **this** hard? Psychology, theology, English, and that most dreaded of all, third year German. I wondered if I would survive my first semester. There was plenty of fun to be had but disappointment as well. I did not make the freshmen basketball team and I rarely dated. Maybe this really wasn't for me after all. Neither of my parents had finished high school and I had no role models for academic perseverance other than my cronies in the dorm. Since we were all similarly situated I didn't think that following their lead was always in my best interest, especially those who rarely cracked a book or made it to class.

After some family time at Christmas break I thought college life just might work out for me. I did have one semester under my belt and I had passed my fearsome German class, albeit with a sorry C-. Ouch! I don't remember getting a grade that low in years. My grade point average no doubt ranked me in a lower echelon, but I am a Cubs fan so hope springs eternal every year that improvement is just around the corner.

Even college is not wholly cerebral, so I found that my tours around campus and to the dining hall did awaken my other senses periodically. No, it wasn't that delectable dining hall cuisine, but there was one waitress who caught my eye. Short, dark hair, she mostly scurried around with trays and occasionally sashayed over to my table. I took notice. Once, on a Sunday afternoon, I was heading back to my dorm when this same vision of loveliness approached me from the other direction. Our eyes engaged, and she flashed her signature smile and said hello as we passed each other by. Hmm, I thought. Who knew this sprite, nattily attired young lady? I figured my next move was to ask around.

Luckily, I found a fellow on my dorm floor who had dated her. "Elaine," he said, "was very nice. I had a good time when we went out. I think you'll like her." That was all that I needed. One positive recommendation beat the alternative: tossing darts at pictures from the freshmen "bod book" as it was known and hoping for the best.

A musical group was coming to campus in a few weeks, so I figured that was a good draw for her if she didn't remember our brief sidewalk encounter sometime earlier. In fact, that might even be more in my favor in case she judged me a dud, she could at least have a good time listening to the music. A brief phone conversation elicited her consent and the date was made. On the appointed night, I picked her up on foot as our dorms were across from each other and we headed over for the concert. I don't remember anything that we talked about that night, but I did like the Ramsey Lewis Trio and I did like her. Although the next steps did not follow a straight line, over the next few months we were a couple. We only lived 2000 miles apart so why should that stop anything?

As the school year was drawing to a close, she told me her parents would be driving out from her home town of Lynden, WA to pick her up and return home for the summer. The meeting went well and now I had met my prospective in-laws without knowing it. There did not appear to be any need for damage control, so we made plans for me to fly out to see her that summer. Never mind that I had never flown before and that it could cost some prohibitive sum to get there. Neither rain nor snow, sleet nor cold, fog or dark of night could hold me back from my appointed travel to that distant region. At that moment I was hooked, and my jaw agreed with the snare.

(This is one of a number of poems that I wrote to Elaine while we were apart during the summers we were in college. This one came to me in 1970 with some help from the beloved Scottish poet, Robert Burns).

My Love is Like a Red, Red Rock

My love is like a red, red rock:

> Solid,
> Thorough,
> Strong,
> Life-giving.

Funny to call love a rock.

> Red like blood,
> the color which gives the color and
> sustenance to life.

Life-giving?

Each day I am given new life when I reflect on you.

I know you are the same.

Together. Soon to be one. A single entity.

True as stone, our hearts and lives are enmeshed

and cannot be separated.

God did a good job

James Vander Kamp

TRANSITIONS

Sometimes I try to think back to my life as a single man. That was long ago and is becoming a smaller portion of my life with each passing year of marriage. My single days were primarily my teens since we married at twenty-one in 1970. High school to college, living at home to living in a dorm, life was moving but I really didn't pay much attention until I met the woman of my dreams and everything changed. Married life meant my first real experience living away from friends and family and our first time having to choose where we would live.

Since we married the summer after our junior year in college, we knew we needed a place when we came back in the fall. We were in school in Grand Rapids, MI and since we had both been in dorms, we really didn't have great familiarity with the city and where we might set up our first abode. We got advice from some friends who had been living off campus and eventually settled on a second-floor apartment in an older part of town.

It was a spacious place with two bedrooms, one of which we made into our study. We thought we were in heaven in that we had a bathroom off our bedroom, a large walk-in closet, large kitchen and a living room, all for the princely sum of $65 per month. There were a few drawbacks but we were confident they would not deter two lovebirds who merely were there to focus on becoming the first in each of our families to graduate from college.

I mentioned drawbacks. First of all, Michigan in late summer was often oppressively hot and humid. Living on the second floor meant that the heat that we got on a given day was there to stay so we sweltered from the start of school until we found some relief in October. I recall that we found an old fan in our closet and thought that a cooling breeze would be just what we needed. When we plugged it in and turned it on for the very first time we had a surprise: immediately sparks flew and we blew a fuse, so our dream of a cooling draft ended abruptly.

Michigan in winter was just the opposite. Ice, snow, and frigid temperatures were our companions for months. Unfortunately, we soon learned that our bedroom was unheated! It was common to see our breath as we climbed into bed and snuggled tightly together as much for survival as for love. The attached bathroom was no better. It had a tub but no shower. Sometimes we would fill it with hot water and leap in, much like living in Colorado where one can go from home to outdoor hot tub and look at the wintry sky. In our case, we looked at the bathroom ceiling, with an occasional visit by a spouse who needed to brush their teeth.

Upon graduation it was time for another move, this time to the far reaches of northwest Washington in the city of Lynden, the land of my wife's family and her first school teaching job. We packed up our '62 Chevy and looked like the ultimate low rider as all our worldly goods filled both the trunk and the back seat and weighed us dangerously close to scraping the ground. Our nearly 2000-mile trip brought us to the Promised Land and a stint living with her parents and two sisters. That interesting time lasted a month and then we thought we had died and gone to heaven. We found a fully furnished house in town with all the accouterments. It even had a color TV, something neither of us had ever had before.

These folks were vacation travelers in retirement who pulled an Airstream trailer to distant locations for many months at a time. They had a son in town who collected the rent, this time the unheard-of total of $30 per month. That won't buy dinner for two these days. The one oddity we encountered was that they slept on twin beds. Although we had slept apart longer than we had slept together, we decided we didn't want to return to that state. Some quick maneuvering and the beds were together and so were we. Marital bliss was ours once again.

We became accustomed to our relatively luxurious surroundings but knew that the departure bell would toll for us all too soon. With a month to go in the school year, we had to move to another location. This time we found a great second story apartment, but it was being painted so we decided to take it a month later while we moved into a significantly lesser place for the one month interim. Our one-month abode featured a kitchen table which had to fold down for eating because the spartan quarters were quite snug. The bathroom was so small that you had to know exactly what you were going in there to do before entering because the space did not allow much room for reconsideration.

Somehow, we survived those cramped quarters and once again had a great reward awaiting. Our new place was above the elderly owners of the building and included two bedrooms, kitchen and a spacious living room with an expansive picture window. That view made life worthwhile. Our place backed up to a large field which abutted the Nooksack River. No homes, no businesses, just pasture and cattle. Elevating one's eyes brought even greater pleasure: The Cascade Mountains were on our horizon including the impressive peak of Mt. Baker, covered in snow year-round. My wife was used to this sight having grown up here, but it changed this mid-western city dweller forever. How could I ever go back to life in the flatlands? Mountains would always be a part of any place we would live in the future, so Colorado was a natural landing place when duty called. We thank God every day that our path led us here.

TURNING POINTS (2)

"Kids"
Here is our brood pictured in 2000: Katie, Andrea, Nate, and
Missy

When I consider my life and the moments of tumult as well as triumph, I am always grateful to God for my children. Each one is a gem and just like a gem, has many different facets that sparkle. Perhaps that's why people often say, "Before you were even a twinkle in my eye, you were designed as that unique, one of a kind person that you are today."

Leaning into Life

As far as I am concerned, there is nothing like being present at the birth of one's children. I was blessed to be there each time a new Vander Kamp came on the scene. From the birth of our one and only son Nathan in 1975 to Kathryn three years later, Melissa in 1981 and our darling third daughter Andrea in 1988, I participated as observer, coach, cheerleader, and overwhelmed husband and father.

Naturally, I must give credit where credit is due: my dear wife Elaine carried each baby and then helped them enter this brave new world with a combination of courage, fear, strength, and joy. For me there was always a mystical quality about child birth, but for her it was practical, painful, and sometimes even punishing.

Our La Maze class at Mercy Hospital during the first pregnancy gave us a way to think about birth that was never previously considered. If a track athlete must be concerned about his breathing while running a race, then all the more for the mother to be. I was taught to be a breathing coach, though if you were to ask me today what I did, I couldn't remember a thing about it. It certainly was both a diversion from the pain and a focus on each phase as we rolled through the birth process.

My joy during each birth was unrivaled. Tears flowed freely as I saw each sticky, crusty little person emerge. We as parents became the King and Queen of cue balls as each baby born was as bald as the last one. Birth was obviously an unforgettable beginning for us as we saw our family grow through the years. This was the time when we trusted God for a miracle and were rewarded in a most magnificent way each time.

What more can one say about seeing one's children born? For me it was an overwhelmingly positive, exciting emotional experience that exceeded jumping off a sixty-foot cliff in Hawaii, ziplining in the Redwoods 150 feet above the ground, or seeing the famed Basilica in Rome by Michelangelo. I am sure I missed a few other high points but truly, seeing one's children born is a transcendent spiritual experience. Thanks be to God for His unspeakable blessing to Elaine and me!

BASEBALL BEEN BERRY GOOD TO ME

(I owe the title to Garret Morris of Saturday Night Live fame who played a fictional former Mets star, Chico Esquela, now retired and doing the sports report for the nightly news. His signature line was "Baseball been berry good to Chico Esquela.")

Here I am with my older brother Dick on a trip to see our forever heroes at Spring training in Arizona.

Sports have always played a big part in my life, particularly my early life. My affinity for sports began at the tender age of nine when I was stricken with the flu. Unable to go to school, I lay on the couch in front of the black and white RCA Victor, watching the World Series between the Milwaukee Braves and the New York Yankees. I had only recently started to play a little baseball myself in the empty lot close to my house so seeing the Big Leagues have at it in 1957 was not just a treat, it was mesmerizing.

There is little specific recall of that series but what it did was seize me for life on the National Pastime. It is hard to comprehend how watching a game for the first time could capture a little boy's imagination, but I was hooked. Baseball became my passion in all its forms, from playing catch in the front of the house with my older brother or our Dad when he came home from work, to playing pick-up games in empty lots or school yards until it got too dark to see, I couldn't get enough of it. We played underhand slow pitch softball and overhand faster pitch baseball with a "league" (short for Major League) hardball. We had mitts that came from all sorts of people and places and we always compared the autograph on the glove to see if it was someone we knew and revered. Surely, the name on the mitt would make us better ball players if it was signed by the right guy!

Growing up in Chicago with two Major League teams was special. The Cubs were the favorites in our house, but the White Sox could get a grudging acknowledgement from time to time because they always had a better record. In 1959 the Sox finally broke through and finished ahead of the Yankees and went to the World Series while the Cubs remained mired in the second division of the National League, despite having the MVP of the league on their team in the person of Ernie Banks. Nicknames were endemic in baseball, so we certainly liked Jungle Jim Rivera, Li'l Looie Aparicio, Smoky Burgess and "Big Klu," Ted Kluzewski, on the Sox, but alas, nicknames were not enough and the newly relocated L.A. Dodgers defeated the local heroes four games to two.

Those formative years in my life, referred to as the latency period by psychologists, were special. Before hormones alerted us to the fact that there were girls all around us and teachers wanted us to pay close attention in school, and we were even required to sing in choirs, we all got caught up in baseball. We knew players by name from both leagues, who were the stars, what their statistics were for home runs, batting average, and runs batted in; who the star pitchers were and how many games they had won; what teams could be counted on to win (the Yankees) and to lose (the Cubs). We memorized records for players from the past and who led in what categories. In many ways, I now see how my interest in doing math in my head came from consuming baseball statistics at an early age which then could be flaunted when someone started a conversation about a player they knew only in a most cursory way.

Little did I realize that I was watching Hall of Fame players when I watched the hapless Chicago Cubs. Ernie Banks, the two-time Most Valuable Player, Ron Santo, all-star third baseman and later broadcaster, Billy Williams, soft-spoken, sweet-swinging man from Whistler, AL and Fergie Jenkins, a black Canadian hockey player who was a frequent 20 game winner, were all brightly shining stars, yet all tasted defeat far more than victory on the fifties, sixties and later teams. I attended games at both Wrigley Field and Comiskey Park. In those days, the Cubs played all their games during the day, so a summer ride on the El train or a rare Saturday with our Dad was within our reach, even though we were living in suburban Oak Park. Though infrequent, these were special times to be savored and remembered long after the ball game ended and the score cards were tallied for posterity.

Baseball was more than a game, however. Little did we know that in playing as young boys we were learning important lessons that would help us throughout life. Captains had to be picked and teams chosen. Being respected by your peers, therefore, was important. People were judging your skill and work ethic. Since our games had no umpires, we had to know the rules, and had to negotiate close calls on the bases and in the field. "Cheaters never prosper" was a standard comment when we felt that we were being slighted. Integrity was important so the game could go on fairly and the outcome not be shrouded in a cloud of doubt.

So, after a lifetime of playing and following baseball, where am I today? Getting ready for the World Series! The Cubs are in it, something that has never happened in my entire lifetime. Excitement, tension, anxiety; what will the outcome be? I will be relishing this edition like none other. Hope springs eternal in the heart of a true fan, especially a Cubs fan.

Post script: The Cubs did win the 2016 World Series in dramatic fashion against the Cleveland Indians. The Series went to game seven and was tied after nine innings. The Cubs won it in the tenth by a final score of 8-7.

Here I am with the World Series trophy! Due to connections our son has with Mr. Tom Ricketts, owner of the Cubs, we were invited to his house for a post-victory celebration, complete with a chance to take pictures with the trophy. It was an unbelievable thrill after so many years of heartache.

James Vander Kamp

ON LEARNING TO WORK

"A hard worker has plenty of food, but a person who chases fantasies has no sense." Proverbs 12:11

"Lazy people want much but get little, but those who work hard will prosper." Proverbs 13:4

In everyone's life there are rites of passage. From a first suit to a first kiss to a first car, all these events bring with them a definition of the event itself, but also a new understanding and meaning for the one experiencing them. Behavior must change as higher expectations now fall on the one who has successfully crossed a boundary.

As a child, I lived blissfully free of responsibility. I was not required to make my bed, but I was conscientious about picking up my clothes and keeping my bedroom neat. No allowance was tied to specific chores (no allowance, period!), so my summer days are thought of fondly as a time of playing and exploring the world in our safe neighborhood.

My mother, on the other hand, was an enterprising sort and thought that her sons should not lay around too much. That meant outside for play or until someone needed a kid for a job. Mine came early, at age 10. Two blocks down the street was a small Mom & Pop grocery, right across from an elementary school. Aptly nicknamed "the school store," they offered a limited array of canned goods and other off-the-shelf items with Ethel behind the counter, a butcher shop handled by her husband Tom, and a multitude of candies, pretzels, ice cream bars and popsicles to entice the hordes who dropped in at the end of the school day.

Since we lived close, my mom wondered if there was ever a need for a youngster to lend a hand around the store. She must have read Tom's mind because in no time I had my first job. I started by picking up all the errant wrappers left behind by the thundering herds, coming in at 5:00 each afternoon and at 2 on Saturday. This year-round position rewarded me handsomely with a shiny half dollar and my choice from the ice cream freezer each week.

I rose in the ranks through the years to burning my daily collection in a pot belly stove in the back of the store, increasing my pay to $1 each week. I stocked shelves with canned goods when the occasional delivery arrived, and I worked for Tom the butcher on Saturdays, cleaning the tools of his trade and mopping up blood from the floor of the cooler where enormous pieces of meat hung on hooks suspended from the ceiling. My pay rose accordingly: $1/week for picking up and burning trash; $.50/hour to stock shelves and an astounding $1.50 for a couple of hours on Saturday.

I stayed working for Tom and Ethel until I graduated high school. In the meantime, however, I supplemented my income with various other enterprises. I did yard work for ladies in my neighborhood. It seemed that one job would often lead to another, as the word spread of my prowess behind a lawnmower or raking leaves in the fall. I also manned a paper stand at a factory where workers could purchase any one of three Chicago dailies when they got off work. The paper cost $.07 in those days and I would ride my bike from school and hawk papers for about an hour before heading the near-two miles back home.

By the time I was 16, I was working on a garbage truck on Saturdays. The 6 a.m. start was a little tough but the $20 payday made it well worth it. It also gave me an urban education as we would traverse the streets and alleys of Chicago and discover some unique, interesting, and surprising venues for trash removal. My horizons expanded to working the same job during holiday school breaks my last two years of high school. I also spent summer days working in a print shop and at a sporting goods store close to home, both positions compliments of my irrepressible mother.

I moved to the big time when I graduated high school. With college in my sights and a modest bank account to get me started, I got a job at Ceco Steel in Lemont, Illinois. My job involved cutting rebar and loading it on trucks where it would be shuttled to construction sites across metropolitan Chicago. I made a union wage without joining the union and learned a little about union politics as well. We punched in at 7 o'clock and worked a six-day week. Since summer was construction season, our plant ran three shifts, round the clock. That meant when they needed extra hands, we did overtime before our regular shift, coming in at 5. Since we had a one-hour commute, I had to roll out of bed around 3:30. So much for the night life of a late teen. When friends would call, I was already in bed. I played on our church softball team those summers and always hoped for the early game, so I wouldn't nod off waiting for my turn at bat.

After three summers at Ceco, we heard change was in the air. It looked like overtime was going to be cut and I was getting married at the end of the summer, so cash was king. Where to turn? I went back to my former career in sanitation engineering but with a new employer. I made my highest wage of all-time, $4 an hour, and had a great time with some hard-working men who would still be doing this long after I finished college.

Leaning into Life

I graduated in four years with no debt and a new wife as we graduated together in 1971. I think that learning to work, learning responsibility, learning to get along with a wide variety of people were perhaps among the greatest things I could have learned in my early years. I thank my parents, especially my mother, for knowing that what I needed was not always what I wanted. I believe I have been able to offer my own children many of those same lessons and I hope the next generation after them will see the value in that message.

James Vander Kamp

OBSTACLES IN MY EARLY CAREER

As a very young man, I had an idealistic streak. When I taught school in Lynden, WA, I wondered why my students weren't as passionate as I was as I tried to impart my accumulated wisdom during 45-minute time blocks. It didn't take long for me to decide that what I really needed was a career change, even though I had only labored for less than two years at teaching, and I had no idea what that new career would be. When in doubt, return for more education.

After completing graduate school, my wife and I latched on to something that attracted us both. A new organization called Roundup Fellowship was forming in Colorado and needed houseparents to live with kids from troubled backgrounds. We applied, interviewed, and moved to Denver in 1974 to begin a job where we felt called and believed we could have an influence on kids who we really knew nothing about.

We took our first boy in March 1975 and were off to the races. Other boys were added, and we began to see what we really didn't know. Two white middle class, somewhat sheltered individuals were now in the role of parenting a house full of teenagers. God help us! Fortunately, I believe He did.

Over the next two and one-half years we had a string of boys come and go and even saw a few stay. Our twins, Lonnie and Ronnie, were among the early kids we had. Sadly, I attended both their funerals as they died much too early, in their 40s, due to serious, neglected health conditions. Chris, Tony, Robert, John, Willie, Troy and many more were our charges. Some of these became lasting relationships and we saw kids grow up and move into careers or, in at least one case, go to prison. I was always thankful for these early years and the strengthening of our marriage as we became a team committed to helping those young men any way that we could.

Looking back, it was obvious that we were ill-equipped to handle the avalanche of situations that came our way on a regular basis. We received virtually no formal training and the expertise we showed, if at all, came from the seat of our pants. In the Sound of Music, Rolf said to Liesl, "You need someone older and wiser telling you what to do. I am seventeen going on eighteen, I'll take care of you." Our age spread with some of our oldest boys was just seven years, so our life experience was hardly what it needed to be in order to provide them with the wisdom required to change some of the unpleasant things that had happened to them during their tender years.

Although our naivete' often worked against us, I think we actually became fairly quick learners. Boys who lied as a way of life only could get by with some things once or twice before we old folks caught on. One situation in this regard stands out vividly. One of our charges came home one day with a watch which he proudly displayed to his fellow housemates. When I quizzed him about his new possession, he assured me that he had bought it at a local store on East Colfax near where we were living.

Since his reputation was hardly sterling, I pressed the matter. He gave me an elaborate explanation of how he mobilized his personal resources to make the purchase. I told him we would go down to that store and verify that the transaction had indeed taken place as he described. We drove over and went in while he maintained his story. When I asked the proprietor if he remembered our young man purchasing a watch, he responded with a rather quizzical look. Our boy tried to remind him how he had come by after school the day before and paid cash for the watch. Within seconds it became abundantly clear that no such purchase had occurred but rather our fellow had taken what was called "the five-finger discount." His brazenness in literally trying to convince the shopkeeper that he had bought the item was a great lesson for me in the future. Pathological lying was a reality I had never encountered before. This experience taught me the lesson that if needed, I should go to the wall to see a situation through so that a life lesson could be taught about truthfulness and honesty as values that everyone should have.

OUR ONE AND ONLY SON

Married life was good. We were young and able to do things at a moment's notice. We enjoyed so many of the same interests that there were few times when we chose to be apart. Still, we knew the day would come, the day when we decided to expand our household and bring in an outsider. For us, that blessed event took place on November 26, 1975 with the birth of our first child and only son. Though we have been blessed with three more children, our son never had a brother.

At the time that Elaine became pregnant, we were working as houseparents in a group home. We had lots of opportunity to practice parenting on other people's kids before our first entered the world. The prospect of having our own child brought us incredible excitement and anticipatory joy. Our own baby – wow! Feelings mean everything at a time like that and we were bursting with expectation.

Those early years were wonderful. We took Nathan everywhere. His first road trip was on a mattress in the back seat of our 1970 Chevy when we drove to see family in Chicago at Christmas. He was a month old and slept most of the way. Fortunately, he has since changed his ways and now rises daily and goes to work as any upstanding adult is supposed to.

A year later we purchased a home and his life with a multitude of big brothers was over. I switched jobs within Roundup Fellowship and we could now concentrate on our own family. Elaine was home with him and each day I would come home wondering what new achievement had occurred and how close our son was to ascending to the U.S. Presidency. Fortunately, that didn't happen, but our joy grew as we went to parks, on bike rides, summer hikes and winter sledding.

James Vander Kamp

As our family expanded, we now faced the prospect of extending our love to another child. Amazingly, we found that built-in capacity to share our love with our daughter Katie while not diminishing the supply left over for our first born. God does give parents many remarkable capabilities but giving love to an increasing brood certainly ranks high on the list. The second child did nothing to change our feelings toward Nate; in fact, we saw that our hearts were growing in capacity to love even more. That is a real blessing.

His early years were filled with firsts: the first to walk, speak, exit diapers, ride a bike, toss a ball, start school and more. For us as parents, those truly were the "wonder years," as in "I wonder what trouble he will get into next?" Thankfully, that never proved to be too much of an issue, although we were never sure if that was due to exquisite parenting on our part or a miraculous act from God above. There is safety in assuming the latter over the former.

I have always relished the role of father. Knowing that I could directly and deeply influence my son brought me a mixture of delight, pride, laughter, and anxiety. Having that type of influence was challenging when I saw him move in a direction I would not have chosen for him and yet brought great pleasure as he got older and began making decisions that were to his benefit and to his family's sublime satisfaction.

There are examples aplenty of both extremes, but a couple stand out. In seventh grade Nate was out with a friend in a Target store. Something on a shelf caught their fancy but exceeded their ability to pay so they decided why not do the next best thing: Nate was chosen to shove the item into his pants as the two of them bid a hasty retreat from the store. "Not so fast, fellas," a security guard said as they were headed to the parking lot for a "clean" getaway. Cameras were the retailer's best friend even then.

He had to not only return the item, but was ordered to pay a fine and attend a class which was supposed to teach him the error of his ways. This was more than a teachable moment and we spent some time discussing not just the incident but what impact this could have on his life down the road. I think it made a proper, lasting, impression.

The other incident was altogether different. When Nate was a sophomore in college and contemplating his major, a moment of truth came which would certainly set a direction for his life. While he was literally in line at registration for his next semester, he called me. He laid out the fact that he was faced with making a choice that would keep him at Calvin College with a limited life prospect, or, if he followed what he saw as his real desire for his future, he would have to stop the registration process and plan on transferring to a school that had what he really believed he wanted for a major and career.

This was a magic adult moment. He told me about the desire of his heart, to get into the fledgling field of computer animation. Calvin gave him a glimpse of the field but couldn't give him a full-blown major. He could transfer to the Art Institute of Colorado and try his hand in a cutting-edge field and see where it might lead. I advised him to follow his heart and mind on this and take the plunge. He switched schools that fall and is happily employed today as a computer animator, making video games for a living.

Now a happily married man with a brood of his own, Nate still faces plenty of moments where he serves as disciplinarian, counselor, coach, and chief decision maker. He learned many lessons at home growing up but we all know that ultimately the choices he makes now are his. We are proud of his accomplishments in his professional life, but even more so in his family life. Having a wonderful companion in Tara makes the journey more pleasurable but good choices are what bring long-term satisfaction. Amen to that.

MY LOVE AFFAIR WITH PERFORMING

"To be or not to be." Hamlet, Shakespeare.

"To dream the impossible dream." Don Quixote, Cervantes

There are many ways people are blessed with self-expression. For some, they have a particularly artistic bent which can be expressed in drawing or painting. Others have wonderful vocal gifts that go far beyond singing in the shower. I have always found my own bent to be toward writing and performing. I use the latter term in a broad sense because for me, being alive and interacting with others has always included an element of performance.

I think this may have started early for me in that my mother told me (and the rest of the family) that when I was a young child, my parents were concerned that I wasn't talking when they thought I should have. In short order after, I did begin, and they wondered if I would ever shut up! Such is the life of a not-so-precocious but give-him-some-time kind of kid.

Elementary school brought with it a few requisite class plays and programs for other students and parents. Even in those early years I do recall beginning my life of wise-cracking and joking, often to the chagrin of the elders in charge. My loud voice carried well beyond the walls of the classroom so that even when our teacher stepped out for a few moments, I was often singled out as the culprit who led whatever uprising had occurred during their absence. This led to some questionable marks on my report cards in conduct. I was most happy when that was dropped as a category when I got to Junior High.

While in high school I was blessed with the opportunity to try out for class plays in my junior and senior years. In both cases, I was given the leading role and realized that this was something that I had been craving all along. I was the Stage Manager in Our Town by Thornton Wilder and played Hjalmar Ekdal in Ibsen's The Wild Duck. My appetite had been whetted. I realized that clowning around in class or with friends was merely a precursor to performing on stage.

College took me a different direction, so I never became a collegiate thespian. It took me a few more years before I realized that I really needed to take another look at some performance options. By the time I took a couple of acting classes I was married with four children. I made a demo tape, had some head shots taken, and got represented by an agent; I was off to the races! I was ready. Actually, what I was ready for was a lot of rejection. Auditions and job possibilities proved to be more tantalizing than titillating. My day job did allow some flexibility so I did go on my share of auditions.

I finally landed my first job: I was in a car commercial, a "Mr. Goodwrench" kind of guy. We shot a thirty second commercial over two Saturdays and about twelve hours and I took home a whopping $150. This is when I also realized I was in this more for the fun than the money but the fun took me a long way. We still needed to eat so I followed the oft repeated adage "Don't quit your day job."

Still, there were a few heady moments along the way. I did several advertisements, voiceovers, and industrial appearances. The latter meant that I was a spokesman for a certain company and had to be particularly believable in order to convince the audience that the wares I was peddling were worthy of purchase. I also got contacted by someone whom I had met along the way who was on the production side of things. He remembered me from some things we had done earlier and told me he was doing a book on tape and wanted me to be the narrator in a romance he was making with a client. There were voice actors for each role and I did everything which was not a role part. I had quite a bit of fun with this over a weekend and we put the money toward a badly needed new mattress. Talk about practical!

This also led me to try my hand at a few community theater projects linking me back to my high school days. This really got my juices flowing. For someone who never sang, danced or played an instrument, I got cast as Captain Von Trapp, the militaristic father of seven in The Sound of Music. This proved to be immensely enjoyable as I had to sing and dance but was spared the chore of learning the guitar. This really is Maria's show and the woman cast into that role was superb. I learned that she had won vocal competitions, while this was the first significant singing I had ever done in my life. We performed before over three thousand folks in the audience and I even had my second youngest daughter play one of my children in the story, a great joy for me.

I did a few other community shows but my formal stage career was relatively short lived. <u>Arsenic and Old Lace</u> and <u>Annie</u> and several Biblical dramas in our church were my main stays, but my agency went out of business within a few years and I did not pursue finding another. I had quite a bit of fun with this during my early forties, but my job had gotten bigger, our family was at a particularly busy stage with teenagers and their many activities, so I decided I needed to focus more on work and family and not pursue acting, at least for a while.

Even though I had a few interesting parts after our kids left the nest, the formal performing phase of my life has probably ended. What all of this made me realize however was that I **am** a performer; I didn't just perform when I got a part in a play or a commercial but being a performer is in many ways who I am. It has allowed me to express myself with more confidence regardless of the situation I found myself in. After all, a performer can always fake what he doesn't really know and if he's convincing enough, he can sell ice blocks to Eskimos. I haven't tried that yet but….

KATYDID, OUR ELDEST DAUGHTER

Becoming parents for the first time is exhilarating, joyful, emotional, and scary. The second time is all the same feelings with a bit of an exception on the scary part. After all, we were now seasoned veterans with three years under our belts. When our little charmer Kathryn came into the world, we now had a child of each sex, so our family was perfect. At the time, we had no idea that two more daughters would follow in subsequent years, but for now, we could bask in the goodness of God in giving us a second "perfect" child.

Katie was a doll with a smiling face and a cheerful demeanor. Some years later, when we began collecting insects as a family activity, we came up with her nickname, Katydid. She didn't exactly chirp, but she was a full participant in everything we did and had a smile that constantly won us over. Her carefree days before she entered school were full of the kind of joy every parent hopes for.

Once school began, we noticed some things that were not what we had planned for. Katydid had a tough time on the learning front, a situation which has persisted throughout her life. At age eleven she had a seizure at school and I was summoned from work to pick her up. She and I talked about what happened and what she remembered. Our next step was a trip to the doctor where we got a diagnosis of epilepsy and a prescription for medication. This has been a lifelong condition for her and something which, on occasion, has been fraught with peril. Seizures are difficult to watch and can appear at the most inopportune times. Her younger years were the most precarious, but epilepsy is a condition that cannot be ignored. Even as an adult, there is a need to make certain that everything is chemically in balance to avoid any breakthrough seizures. Thankfully, that had been case for her for many years. She did experience one in late 2017 while changing medications, but our prayer is that she is now back on the right path and will be able to function on a seizure-free basis for years to come.

Despite various learning difficulties and some social awkwardness, certain positive things emerged as well. Katie became an intensely loyal and compassionate person, not demanding or sulking despite often being excluded by other girls in her class. When she developed a friendship, it was taken seriously. This has helped her become a surprisingly resilient person. She is someone to be counted on for support through thick or thin.

By the time she went to high school, her pattern included a spotty academic record as well as limited success in sports and artistic endeavors. Those years were stressful, but she did find a niche on the track team as a distance runner. That led to some solid friendships and quite a few exceptional moments when her two-mile relay team challenged and then consistently broke the school record for that distance. If there was a time to shine for Katie, it clearly came as she careened around the track, baton in hand, stretching toward her teammate to make the pass that would give them another victory.

Graduation from high school was a time of great joy for her because it meant an end to mandatory academics that were such a strain. Her love of children led her into what has become a career for her: working in the child care/pre-school arena. Unlike many of her classmates, she jumped into the workplace immediately upon graduation. This move also shaped her as she had to form a new identity as a working woman at a relatively tender age. The tale of her first child and our first grandchild has a prominent position elsewhere in this memoir (see "The Next Generation").

Being a single mom, Katie had a few resources that others in her situation may not have had. She lived at home with parents and sisters who cared deeply about her and her new arrival. We believe that the situation with her then ten-year-old sister Andrea is instructive. Elaine and I were initially traumatized when we learned that we were expecting when we were soon to turn forty. Naturally, the joy of our baby quickly wiped out any misgivings we had about having her later in our lives. Fast forward to the birth of our first grandchild. Little did we realize that what **seemed** like such heartache for us some years earlier, would become such a blessing for Katie. She now had a willing babysitter at the ready to relieve her of her round-the-clock responsibility of baby care (her own) and child care (her job). God knows far better than we when we make plans for ourselves and our future.

Less than five years later, wedding bells rang for Katie and Luke and a new episode began. An apartment, a home, another baby, and a move to another city, all were part of the whirlwind of their early years of marriage. Part of that included Grandma Elaine homeschooling both of their children for a few years prior to their move to Greeley. This solidified intergenerational relationships and set the stage for an unexpected return to Denver to live with us in 2016, while they worked to get themselves back to a firmer financial footing. They are succeeding in that regard and hope to move to their own place sometime in mid-2018.

One other important point for Katie. While working again in the pre-school/day care arena, Katie was confronted with the fact that she would have to get more formal education to maintain her employment. Considering her earlier educational experiences, this was not something she looked forward to. After a year of intensely hard work, including many hours at night and on weekends, she passed with flying colors and received her credential. She was rewarded with congratulations by family members who knew what a difficult road this was for her and what a great accomplishment it was.

We are proud of her for being diligent in the face of difficulty and being willing to take on a task that has historically been unpleasant. We are blessed by her and know that blessings await her as she and her family anticipate some exciting changes in the future.

Leaning into Life

THE NATURAL WORLD: GOD'S CREATION

"Let the heavens rejoice and let the earth be glad; let the sea roar and all its fullness. Let the field be joyful and all that is in it. Then all the trees of the woods will rejoice before the Lord." Psalm 96:11-12.

I have always had an affinity for the outdoors. Growing up in the Midwest, we experienced all four seasons and found joy in each. When spring sprang we were ready to shed heavy coats and long johns for regular pants and lighter jackets. Summer meant no school, baseball, swimming pools and bike rides. By the time Fall came with shorter days and a return to school, we grudgingly accepted. The blast of winter meant sleds, snow forts, snowball fights and the holidays we loved: Thanksgiving, Christmas, and New Year's. That rhythm of life offered order, balance, and something to look forward to every few months.

Along the way, I finally realized what God had given me: a created world that was chock full of wonder and worthy of exploration. Whether it was the uniqueness of each snowflake (my mother said no two were alike), the fragrance after a spring rain, the times spent catching crickets and lightning bugs, or the dazzling array of colors in the fall, there was always something that drew me in, always something that captured my attention and imagination.

I always loved bike rides as a boy. They literally transported us away from the homes and businesses which we knew so well and brought us to lovely stretches of meadows, ponds, and forests. This was a precursor to formalizing some of my outdoor experiences, when school projects demanded leaf

71

and insect collections. From the first time I began looking closely at the variety of trees we had in our neighborhood, I became lost in the unique diversity each leaf offered. This was more than a science project; it was a glimpse into the creativity of God Himself.

From leaf collecting in 7th grade, we moved on to insects the next year. With a magnifying glass in one hand and a jar for my specimens in the other, I joined the hunt. What a spectacle! From monarch butterflies to cutworm moths, from ground beetles to June bugs, from Mormon crickets to those who professed no faith in particular, I caught them all and pinned them neatly on the Styrofoam sheet I got from F.W. Woolworth. Little did I know that these excursions into the wilderness in my youth would prepare me for a repeat performance when my own children came on the scene.

Those Midwestern experiences in the flatlands were nothing compared to the joys I experienced after meeting my wife-to-be and traveling to Washington to see her and meet her family. They were hardy hikers and naturally thought that this city boy needed some exposure to mountains. When we traveled up to Mt. Baker and I saw snow in summer, I was beside myself. Towering hemlocks and spruces, rushing streams and natural snow caves were enough to whet my appetite for more. I knew that the only kind of "more" that would satisfy would be a permanent change of habitat. We moved there after college and then came to Colorado three years later. We have never looked back.

The outdoors replenishes me in so many ways. Colorado is blessed with an abundance of sunshine so everything we look at is through its gleaming lens. Summer means hiking to places old and new. That often includes some time in the supine position looking at the billowing clouds above. Autumn beckons with its Siren call to see quaking aspens arrayed in all their golden splendor. When snow falls, the hills call out for skiing and breathtaking views. I am in my element. Creation is alive. Let the trees of the fields clap their hands as I join them in giving thanks to God for His wondrous majesty.

James Vander Kamp

AN ODE TO TREES

I have always liked looking at trees.
From the broad-shouldered oak in my son's backyard
to the newly sprouted blue spruce my parents had,
I have always liked looking at trees.

My sister has a dizzying variety at her house.
After ten years on their eighty acres
she now boasts maples and oaks that
are approaching their prime,
poplars and cottonwoods and even a gingko.
I love to say, "gingko."
It has a magical leaf that defies comparison
with most pedestrian tree leaves.
I have always liked looking at trees.

She has two weeping willows that,
when seen from afar,
are really bent over, crying into the pond
on which they are planted.
I have always liked looking at trees.

My brother's neighborhood has sycamore trees.
I don't remember ever seeing a sycamore before.
I only remember a diminutive tax collector named Zaccheus
who climbed a sycamore because he was too short to see Jesus.
I bet he liked trees too but for a different reason than I.

I must admit that I don't like every kind of tree.
You can have the Russian Olive,
that thorny tree with a pale leaf and a too-short life span.

Leaning into Life

I don't like looking at the Russian olive but
I have always liked looking at trees.

I have blue eyes and my wife says I look good in blue.
My favorite color, though, is green.
Luscious, deep, bold, shiny green.
I think I know why.

Because I have always liked looking at trees.

James Vander Kamp

MELISSA JOY, AS IN JOYFUL

"O, the joy!" Meriwether Lewis upon seeing the Pacific Ocean
for the first time.

Our life was moving along at an agreeable pace. After
five fun childless years, we thought maybe it was time to start
a family. Nathan came first, followed by sister Katie three
years later. Not much was spoken about expanding the brood
until I began broaching the subject with my dear wife. "More
kids?" she responded, somewhat incredulously. "We already
have a perfect family, a boy and a girl. Why more?" "I
thought you would like a larger family," I replied. We both
came from families of four children; surely one more would
not be too many. I pressed the issue until my lovely bride
relented and agreed to make the appropriate adjustments that
might make a third pregnancy possible, Lord willing.

The stage was set, and after some difficulty getting
pregnant, the announcement could finally be made: we were
pregnant. Our custom was never to inquire in advance
regarding the sex of our children and we held the line on that
plan. We liked the idea of being surprised when the youngster
popped out. Since we already had a boy and a girl, we thought
the addition of either would be just fine. Low and behold, June
15, 1981 brought us our second girl, Melissa Joy Vander
Kamp.

None of our children were particularly large or small at
birth so having a seven-pound girl seemed just about right. A
year later we wondered if she was growing normally as she had
gained a scant ten pounds. The doctor did a full skeletal x-ray
to assure us that she was okay but just a bit small for her first
year of life. In addition, the blond locks of her siblings were

conspicuously absent on her. Alas, the shiny pate that was a characteristic of all our children at birth remained with Missy well beyond her first year.

As our beloved pipsqueak grew, we did notice that hair and physical size were not her defining features. Once she found her voice it seemed that speech would carry the day: she was a yakker. From pre-school to elementary, there were few quiet moments. She was bright, happy and eager to learn.

One day we noticed an announcement for a Parlor Poetry Recitation contest at a local library. Missy loved to learn and could memorize things easily so we showed up for the contest with the entire family in tow. She wore a quaintly styled dress and had a bow somehow attached to her thin blond hair. As a kindergartener, she was by far the youngest contestant but was also by far the most eager and effervescent. When her turn came she breezed through her well-memorized poem and now all we could do is wait for the judges' choice of a winner. From our point of view as proud parents, the outcome was never in doubt: the certificate of honor went to our beaming daughter. This would be the start of many drama roles Missy would play through her middle school years.

Besides reciting, Melissa took on acting roles at church and school, some which included singing. We even got her into a dance class, where as a nine or ten-year-old, she was doing a little soft shoe with a hat and cane. Needless to say, we were very proud parents. She did well in school and got involved in sports including basketball, baseball and volleyball.

What we always saw in her was a happy, joy-filled, fun-loving person. She loved to read and would drive us crazy in the summer by staying up well beyond any sensible person's bedtime devouring an entire series of books by a particular author she liked. High School brought her beauty and boys, dates to proms and homecoming events, and a ready acceptance into college.

College life was filled with good friends for a lifetime and some exceptional opportunities for study abroad. She spent a semester in Spain and a month in Mexico to give her two very different Spanish-speaking experiences for her major. She did well and graduated in 2003. Along the way, she had a most serendipitous and providential meeting with a man from Long Island, New York while attending a college party. She moved to Long Island where she had procured a job after graduation, speaking Spanish to recent immigrants who were applying for insurance through Suffolk County Social Services. Although, she and her suitor saw each other regularly, nothing monumental occurred so she decided to move back to Denver. He followed sometime later and the wooing continued.

Wedding bells rang in 2006 but before that we had many heart-to-heart discussions about what she saw in Todd, a man more than ten years older whose entire family lived on the island. Those were clarifying moments for us and no doubt for her as well. It is always good to have your head on straight when you will be making life's big decisions. Hers is squarely fixed on her shoulders.

The marriage years led to the birth of two darling little girls and then, a moment of truth: should they try for a third? This was reminiscent of her parents' process in deciding to try to expand our clan. As a career woman in the insurance industry, this was no small decision, especially with the age differential between them as parents. In this case, the caution light switched to green and a delightful little man emerged to join their family. Praise God for good decision-making and good health!

The fact that God blessed them with that third baby is indicative more about their conscious process and their recognition that family carries the day. They love those three little people and only wish that they could spend more time with them. That is as it should be. Melissa Joy is indeed joyful to be around.

[A post-script: Missy is a rational planner in addition to being a fun-loving person. She has confided to me that she is more like me than she ever thought she would be. I take that as a compliment, knowing that kindred spirits, including our own flesh and blood, make life all the sweeter].

POST-MORTEM LETTER TO MOM

Dear Mom,

It has taken me some time to get around to writing this but I think I needed that time. You see, when you died I really wasn't able to put my thoughts into words; it was just too quick for me to pen my thoughts. Time to reflect has been both healing and percolating. I really believe that I can now offer you some honesty, respect, and love based on my lengthier reflection.

Leaning into Life

I do remember a little about my early childhood, though it is obvious that many details have dropped out. You loved us and you were fun-loving, even though our ideas of fun did not always coincide with yours. I remember you telling us stories from your childhood, from being placed in a barrel by your Dad so he could keep track of his children, to hitchhiking to school with your sisters and girlfriends. I'm sure there was more but most of it escapes me now.

I guess what stays with me the most is your commitment to family and friends. From your lifelong friends in "the gang" to the long-term female friendships in your "Club," there always were people around who we got to know. We always saw aunts, uncles and cousins throughout the year. Even though your mother remarried after grandpa died and moved far away, she remained an integral part of the family when she came back after the loss of her second husband. That could only be true because you were interested in keeping the family flame burning. No doubt that is why all of us, your children, have kept the faith with one another. Your example, in this regard, was a powerful one.

Clearly, you were always a hard-working, driven person. Whether at home with us when we were young or when we got to high school and you were working full-time at National Tea, we always knew we were important to you and Dad. We were allowed to make choices on our own and had freedom to go around the neighborhood but always within the reasonable limits that you set. I don't think you worried too much about us when we were out because you really drilled an ethic of responsibility into all of us.

I suppose to make that work, you offered a plethora of aphorisms to us to guide us through life. "Don't follow the crowd" was a favorite that cautioned us to not join the herd. "Don't be a deadhead" was meant to get us out, participating in school activities or other things in the neighborhood. "Make something of yourself" was another that stayed with me as I moved through high school, college and a career where I finally realized that I had actually practiced what you had preached. Your example was always there for us to see as well so we really couldn't blame you if we deviated from the instructed course.

There was some turbulence along the way too. I was not an angel, so for me the straight and narrow proved to be more circuitous. I stepped off the path, often without you ever finding out. I am quite glad about that. After all, we did grow up in the era when a belt could be applied to the backside for a swifter and more direct punishment rather than grounding or the more recent timeout. Psychology in the fifties and sixties had not yet been introduced into our house. I did feel the lash on a few occasions but I never saw you or Dad as abusive. This actually wrought within me a healthy respect for your authority since I understood that punishments I received were justified and not arbitrary. Thank you for that.

My plan in writing to you was not so that I would exhaustively catalogue your virtues or decry your deficiencies. You were someone who I was proud of and who I loved. Sadly, we were never a very expressive family when it came to showing affection or expressing love. I realize now that I missed out on that when I was home but I never wanted to miss out on that with my own children and grandchildren. Both you and Dad became more expressive when grandchildren came and I knew that our children needed to know you both as the caring, loving people you actually were.

Thank you again for showing me the way to live. The

book of Proverbs says that one should "train up a child in the way he should go, and when he is old he will not depart from it." You certainly did your part in that text. I hope and pray that I have done mine as well.

I love you, Mom.

Jim

James Vander Kamp

MEMORABLE CHARACTERS:

People who shaped me through the years

When one considers the breadth of one's life beyond merely its length, many thoughts come to mind. Surely, we are all products of our experiences and the places we have lived, but even more so, the people who have touched us. Birth families, extended families, neighborhoods, friends, schools, workplaces, all of these have a hand in who we become. Those influences may have been episodic, geographically bound, or life-long relationships that knew no restricted time or space.

I have enjoyed a full life, but I recognize that all relationships are not created equal: childhood, adolescence, adulthood, singleness or marriage, all carry something different by way of influence. As I move into older adulthood I now have the kind of perspective that only years can bring. At the risk of excluding many who I could (or should) have included, I want to present a few characters who helped shape my life, character, and outlook through the years.

As a boy, I had a lot of freedom in my neighborhood but I did have one constant: work. One man stands out during those formative years. **Tom Weilgus**, along with his wife Ethel, owned a small Mom & Pop store two blocks down the street from my boyhood home in Oak Park. I went to work for Tom when I was 10 and moved through a succession of jobs for him until I graduated high school. These were mostly small jobs for small money but I did learn the value of work: be on time, do your job, do it well, learn new things and spend some time philosophizing about life. We both did the former things but he concentrated on the latter as the years passed. I owe him a great deal because I learned about responsibility which reinforced the teaching I received at home. Thanks, Tom.

I had many uncles in my family but one has always stood out: **Uncle Benny Essenburg**. It was okay to include a "y" at the end of most kids' names, but we even had a few that carried over into adulthood and his was one. He married my Dad's sister Grace, and they always were a part of family get-togethers as both families were expanding in the '50s and '60s. He was articulate (he went to Moody Bible Institute later in life and became a pastor), funny, a great story teller (just ask him about people from his workplace), and insightful into many areas of life. This – his insight - is something that I valued increasingly as I got older. The last time I saw him was at my mother's funeral. He is in his 90s now and is the Last of the Mohicans among my uncles. He is cherished by me for his strong spiritual leadership when I was an early adolescent in our boys' club at church and his magnetic personality that attracted people of diverse backgrounds throughout his life. You are a hero to me, Uncle Benny.

Al Vander Dyke makes this list because he showed up in multiple venues during an important period of my life, roughly ages 15 – 20. My older brother worked for his father and we all attended the same church. Al was the player-manager of our church softball team so many summer nights were spent sweating in the sweltering heat and humidity of a mid-western evening, scurrying around the base paths and chasing fly balls in the outfield. Slow pitch softball in the Chicago area was serious business and Al got that message across. In those few years I went from riding the pine to being an All-Star to winning a championship. We developed great camaraderie as a team and many of us had our moments of glory but Al kept us on track and in the game.

Along the way I worked for him as a helper on the garbage truck he owned. I saw Chicago from a very different vantage point when we would go out in the dark and have downtown stops at 5 a.m. on a Saturday and see usually bustling streets virtually deserted. Thank you, Al, for keeping my feet firmly planted on the ground when other kids my age were losing focus instead of gaining it.

It is common for one creating a list such as this to include one's mother or father. For some this might be obligatory so as not to seem ungrateful, while for others it is genuinely heartfelt. In my case, including **Dad** has been a work in progress as I tried to figure out where he fit. Like fine wine he has improved in my assessment as the years have passed. Mark Twain is credited with the statement, "When I was eighteen I didn't think my father knew anything. By the time I reached 21, I was surprised by how much he had learned." How true. As I advanced through college into territory his 10th grade education had never traveled, I was amazed by the wisdom he displayed. His unrelenting positive outlook, humility and thankful attitude set him apart from most of the other "high achievers" I knew. His generous heart filled with love for his children and grandchildren remain an example for me to follow as I now am the patriarch in my own family. I thank God that he made us father and son, a Dad I will always look up to and strive to emulate.

When I moved 2000 miles away from my family to Elaine's hometown, I was a bit unsettled. A newlywed living in a mostly rural small town, I was about as comfortable in my new surroundings as a fish who was asked to climb the nearest pine tree. I was at loose ends even after getting a teaching job and trying to get acquainted in a well-established faculty. Though they were welcoming, and many became good friends, one man stands out: **Pete Bulthuis**.

Pete was a Chicagoan by birth and we shared an urban background, a sense of humor, and a deep desire to touch the lives of our students. His children were in our age category, including a daughter who was a classmate of my wife. He and his wife had an added dimension to their lives, having served in a missionary school in Nigeria for a number of years prior to joining our faculty.

I spent a lot of time with him that year and learned that teaching is about connecting with each student in his or her own unique way. I think I learned that one needed to strive to influence the heart as well as the head and that the classroom could only take students so far. In any case, Pete, you were probably as much a father figure as you were a colleague and now, in retrospect, I'm grateful for the role you played in the formative stage of my brief teaching career.

In 1974 Elaine and I moved to Denver to join a fledgling enterprise, Roundup Fellowship. We were hired to be house-parents in a group home for boys. We were both excited about the opportunity and confident that we were following God's leading. How tough could this be? We were both experienced teachers, I had a newly minted Master's degree in sociology, and our hearts were in the right place. The people who hired us seemed smart, motivated, and committed so what did it matter that they offered no formal training before sending us into a lion's den filled with teenagers.

In short order, we were introduced to **Jim Lane** who would soon become our mentor and trusted friend. Jim and his wife Charlene had started out with some foster kids and soon expanded to their own group home with 12 local urchins. [Note the name game: Jim & Elaine pairing up with Jim & Charlene Lane, a wonderful aside in our new-found life together]. It was from them, but particularly Jim, that we were taught the ropes of being house-parents. Jim was a man who exuded authority and it was from him that I began to see a much larger picture of what we were getting into.

Some years later we were informed that Jim had committed suicide. Despite a large and giving heart, he also had some vexing things that finally took him away. I had great respect for the man who showed me that caring for children could be a way of life. Thank you, Jim, for your wisdom and strength of character that set an example that I could follow throughout my career.

I would be remiss if I did not include my former pastor **Charles Blair**, whose preaching and teaching I sat under for 30 years. I can honestly say he was the greatest preacher I have ever heard because each week he brought something fresh and new and challenging. I grew as a Christian in my faith and as a person in my relationships with others on many levels. I learned about being transparent about my weaknesses and failures. I learned that failure is an experience, not a person. I learned that I could share my life with others on an intimate basis and that others could trust me in the same way.

Thank you, Pastor Blair, for helping me solidify my walk of faith and providing many enduring examples of how one ought to live.

I met **Michael Pass** when our boys were kindergarteners. A group of parents in Park Hill came together to start a new soccer team. I knew little about soccer and nothing about anyone present but was attracted to one larger-than-life character. I found out he was a social worker in private practice who had a number of wide-ranging ideas. Those boys stayed together as a team through eighth grade and my relationship with Michael went far beyond that.

Michael was an over-the-top transplant from New York. He had a winsome personality but did not always exhibit the best of boundaries. A lunch date with him could involve his fork on my plate without a request for permission to sample my dish. He also told me about a cross-dresser he was counseling that almost sent him over the edge and into a new profession.

After working with him on a few joint training projects, he began asking questions about faith. He had started attending a downtown Episcopal Church and appeared to be reading the Bible quite a bit. He and I would discuss various passages until one day he told me he was going to be baptized. Elaine and I attended this event which was obviously an emotional, spiritual experience for Michael.

Fast forward a few years and we were told that his wife Susan had an aggressive cancer that was certain to bring an early end to her life. Sometime during her battle, Michael became ill and was hospitalized. Their adult children, a daughter and son, were obviously distraught and began spending as much time as they could with their parents. I visited Michael in the hospital and he talked about his condition, his family, and the state of his soul. He asked me to pray for him and I obliged, holding the big man's hand and hearing his affirmative murmurings while I prayed. He died within a few days of our visit and his wife followed him all too soon thereafter. What a blow to their kids!

Michael, you were a singular person in my life because I got to know you in a number of contexts as an involved parent, a loving husband, an insightful professional, and a man who came to faith later in life. I always appreciated your erudition, your sense of humor, and your candor. You were a big man who taught me to think bigger regarding my own professional life and sphere of influence. For all of that I thank you and regret that our time couldn't be longer.

ANDREA OUR SHINING STAR

Andrea, daughter number three, child number four, came to us later in life. Although not quite like Abraham and Sarah, still our wait between Missy and our newest darling was considerable. She was indeed a joy as we were more laid back and found ourselves doting on her as she navigated a world which included three older siblings who loved her but who also may have had a whisper of resentment toward this dainty-come-lately.

As we had done with our other children, we wanted to give her a taste of a variety of experiences. Her thick curly locks always were a hit with me as we often found ourselves out and about with a diminishing brood as the years passed. Playing on our swing set was a stark contrast to older brother who was off to college and older sisters who were caught up in the high school scene. After stints in soccer, piano, drama and other artistic pursuits, we finally came to something serious: softball. At 11, Andrea knew nothing of the National Past-time and I was determined that she would finally get to know the game I loved and lived for as a boy.

The coach assigned to this motley lot was amazing. He was a teacher of the game and instilled interest, involvement, and excitement at every turn. Playing catch was not just something you did to warm up. Swinging a bat, even when no ball was pitched, was not merely an exercise. Everything that was done had a genuine purpose and was approached with a sense of seriousness that transcended the tender years of the girls he was mentoring.

The season proved to be a delight to players and parents alike. The coach always told the girls, "Don't ask me the score, just get out there and play hard." This mindset resulted, on more than one occasion, in the young ladies not knowing if they had won or lost at game's end. This proved to be invaluable as the season progressed and the girls grew in skill, grit, and confidence.

There were two memorable games for me as spectator and parent. To qualify for the championship game, they had a rigorous foe to defeat. Andrea had shown her mettle throughout the year and had been elevated in the lineup to the coveted lead-off spot for her ability to make contact, get on base, and often steal her way around the diamond.

With the score tied in the final frame, Andrea led off with a walk. She advanced to second on a steal and to third on a ground out before coming home on a ground out to tie the score and send the game into extra innings. History was made the next inning when a teammate hit a home run to vault the team into the championship game.

A week passed before the faithful assembled at City Park for the big game. The girls from our team were abuzz because they had heard that their opponents had their pitchers all attend "Pitching School." I assumed that meant that those girls were highly skilled in delivering their pitches with speed and precision and that opposing players should appropriately quake as they came to bat.

Here is where our coach again won the day. He told our girls that they were entirely capable of hitting anything that was thrown up to them if they merely applied all the lessons they had learned throughout their successful season. They were in the championship game because they had handled everyone else up to this point and he had no doubts that they could handle this team as well. He exhorted them to play their best and pull for each other and know that they would do just fine.

The game itself was very competitive with neither team gaining much of an advantage. Yes, the girl on the hill showed that she had been to Pitching School with her fast delivery and pitches that rarely strayed from the strike zone. But our girls were up to the task and the game was tied as we entered the fateful final frame.

Andrea was our first batter. As families and friends held our collective breath on the sideline, she delivered a blistering line drive through the box on the first pitch. We all knew the coach's philosophy, so we knew he was instructing her to steal on the very next pitch. She obliged and was now at second. Our batter fanned under the wilting speed of the girl from Pitching School. One out. Andrea took off again when our next batter came up and the pitch got away from the catcher and went to the backstop. She was safe at third with one out. Our next batter came through with a hit and Andrea scored the lead run to give us a 10 - 9 advantage. That would have to hold us over as the opposition batted for the final time hoping to overcome our tenuous one run lead.

Fortunately, our pitcher possessed some wiles of her own and induced the three batters she faced to all hit ground balls back to her where she tossed each one out at first. What a game - what a season! From an untried group of eleven and twelve-year-old girls, some of whom had never played before, to champions celebrated by siblings, parents and grandparents. A night to remember for Andrea and our entire family.

Even though she had many other moments to remember on stage, in choir, and throughout her high school and college career, I will always treasure her time as one of "The Girls of Summer." Thankfully, her story did not end there. My earlier reference to "high school and college" included graduations from both. Her young adulthood included a series of part-time jobs cobbled together to make a full-time income and a stint in her own apartment in Capitol Hill with two roommates. This was a particularly joyful time for her as she had friendships, independence, and the life of a cosmopolitan city dweller for a year.

It was during that year she worked as a "fellow" in a classroom for Denver Public Schools. This was a great experience for her, though it was a bit outside of her desired position. It did imbed a stronger feeling, however, in her desire to be a part of the educational process for some rather needy kids.

Fast forward a bit and she met or perhaps re-met Kevin. They knew each other but it was only after they both participated in the wedding of some friends that the flicker of attraction began to grow. We were overjoyed when the wedding bells chimed, and we are sure that they are well on their way to a life together rooted in love of God and each other and any other little people that may come along.

LIFE HIGHLIGHTS: EXPERIENCE IS KING

It is hard to catalogue the high points in one's life. There are just too many. Certainly, births and weddings always take a lofty position along with the compelling human interactions and interchanges that have drawn us in so many times that they cannot be recounted. I can't imagine putting any particular thing or object on such a list. For me, life has been full of memorable experiences. These typically are what I would call "mountain top" experiences, those things which have stayed with me through the years and are always available for almost instant recall. I have had my share and want to let you know some of the things that have stayed with me over the years.

Although a list like this can't really be presented in a specific order, I feel I must begin with my leap from a cliff on Oahu. Hawaii is paradise virtually anywhere you go in the islands. We went there with some friends in 1997 and enjoyed hiking, swimming and boating all over Oahu. After snorkeling at Hanauma Bay, we drove up to a point where we disembarked from our car and headed to a point high above the crashing waves below. How high were we? It was impossible to tell since we hadn't climbed up to this point but drove up in cork screw fashion to reach our destination. My plan from the beginning was to take the proverbial flying leap into the boisterous foaming brine below.

Lady Macbeth told those around her to "screw your courage to the sticking place," and that is exactly what I had to do. With a photographer below to record my act of bravery – or foolishness, as my wife told me – I set sail on the greatest thrill of my life, and lived to tell about it.

As a younger man, I led a group of teenage boys from Roundup to a flat top mountain above Golden. There we took turns connecting a 100 foot line to the back of a van and then onto a harness fastened securely to each person brave enough to go for a flight. We used an open parachute on each boy's back which we held out so the wind would fill it and then we drove the van as each young man was lofted into the air. The ride didn't last long as our driving course was limited but it was accentuated with squeals of delight.

I took a turn with the other adult along driving. Since I was a heftier object, it took a little running behind the van until the wind did its job. Once off the ground, I flew to the full length of the rope in a second. What a thrill! Looking below and taking in the surroundings added to my ecstasy but the ride ended far too quickly. Flying free and high worked for me.

While on the subject of high flight, I have to include the fabulous zip-line jaunt we took in the redwoods of northern California. As a planned break in the conference I was attending near Santa Cruz, we took to the tall trees at Mt. Hermon Conference Center and sailed our way from station to elevated station. The forest we were in featured trees approaching 400 feet tall and our course was laid out at the 150 feet level. Don your helmet, put on your gear, and away we go! Here is where exhilaration could become intoxication: the freedom to glide through the trees while taking in the entire landscape made Rocky the Flying Squirrel look like a piker. This is a risk I would always recommend.

A different type of high flight is what I love in the

mountains of my adopted state of Colorado: skiing. For anyone who has had cabin fever during a long winter inside, the great outdoors is just the antidote. I skied for the first time when I was 25 and have loved it ever since. Injuries have slowed me down in recent times but skiing remains a constant highlight over the years for me.

I don't want to overlook something I barely touched on above, snorkeling. Whether in Hawaii, Mexico, or Curacao, snorkeling is always a thrill. I have had a number of opportunities to snorkel over the past 40 years and each time I come away with a new sense of wonder for the denizens of the deep. From the gorgeous variety of color and style of coral to the effortless flapping of a sea turtle, to the ominous look of a sting ray, eel or octopus, it is hard to imagine a more gratifying water adventure than using a mask and breathing through a skinny tube. Being up close and personal literally transports me from my terrestrial existence to an aqua experience that is nonpareil.

We have been blessed to travel to many places over the years, both within this country and beyond its borders. For all the natural beauty we have here at home, I still have to give a superlative nod to Italy. Our trip there in 2012 put us in places we thought we could only know through books and movies. Visiting the great cathedrals of Rome and Florence often left us speechless. The beauty, the serenity, the historical value, the sacredness, all overwhelmed us and continue to overwhelm me today. Visiting the unmatched Uffizi Museum next to the Ponte Vecchio on the Arno River in Florence and seeing the Coliseum and its surrounding palace and columns in Rome leave me with a sense of awe for those who lived so long ago. Da Vinci, Michelangelo, Raphael, Donatello, Bernini, and their ilk were indeed gifted masters of sculpture, painting and architecture. They along with the other "lesser lights" have given us a world of art that continues to inspire awe hundreds of years after their work was finished. The Sistine Chapel remains an incomprehensible marvel of unrivaled beauty and mastery that could only have been accomplished through the inspiration of God Himself.

Since this is about personal highlights I will end on a note that can't compare to the grandeur of Italy but was a great thrill for me nonetheless. In 2004 our entire family, 28 members of the Vander Kamp clan, traveled to Curacao in the Netherlands Antilles, compliments of my Mom. If being mesmerized by such a gift that we could share with our entire family wasn't enough, the resort contained a unique feature that put this trip into our highlight reel: a circus area. Yes, we did fly high on the daring trapeze! Many of us, myself included, had the rarest of opportunities to climb the ladder to a small platform, grab the bar, and swing out over the net below. I even did the one trick we were taught, flipping over and hanging by my legs. I couldn't get enough of it.

Despite my advancing years, I hope that I will be able to add to this list in the future. For me, life is always about being willing to take a risk, whether leaping off a cliff or visiting a foreign country where we knew no one. If there is one thing (and I trust that there are more), I have always desired for my own children and grandchildren, it is to be willing to take a risk in life. The rewards typically outweigh the alleged concerns and you will be a better person for trying.

TURNING POINTS (3)

Those who know me know I had an exceptionally long career working for one organization, Roundup Fellowship. I was there for just over 40 years (40 years, 6 months to be exact) including the last 36 as Executive Director. Despite my loyalty and longevity, I did have times when I thought that a change might be beneficial.

Periodically I would come across an advertisement about another organization far away who was looking for a new CEO. There was some method to my madness. It wasn't 100% motivated by a desire for change but sometimes due to circumstances in our family life. My wife lost both her parents in the early eighties at fairly-young ages, which put us in a bit of a tailspin. Our children were young, and we now had only one set of grandparents. That gave us pause as we began to consider whether we should relocate nearer to my parents as they were aging.

I applied for a position in Joliet, Illinois in 1985 at Guardian Angel Home. This venerable institution had been around since just after the Civil War as an orphanage and had reinvented itself as a residential treatment center for troubled teens, something I knew very well. I had planned to visit my family so we could be together to watch the highly touted Chicago Bears in the Super Bowl in January and I was offered an interview that week.

I hit it off very well right from the start with the man I was potentially replacing. Nick was affable and very open about the position and the state of the organization. He showed me around and we talked at length about what the position entailed. I was invited back the next day for a more formal interview with some key staff and a board member.

When I returned I was a bit taken aback by a room full of people. Eleven people assembled to ask me a host of questions about my background, my beliefs, my values and how I would approach the position. After that experience, we discussed some of their plans for the future and I drove back to my parents' home. I left that evening to return to Denver with my head full of thoughts about what I had been through and what prospects I might have in securing the job.

This obviously made for many contemplative moments over the next week as I discussed my reactions and feelings about Guardian Angel with Elaine. Was this the right step for our family? Would a move to the Midwest achieve the goal of improving proximity to family that we both agreed was important to us? Would the disruption be tolerable for all of us to gain a desired end? Was the timing good for my current employer to find a replacement? And last, but not least, would I even be seen as a serious candidate for this job?

As we wrestled with all of this, a call came. The friendly current Director told me that after looking at 26 candidates, I was in the final three. Could I come back for another round of interviews? I told him I would call him back the next day. The moment of truth was upon us. We prayed, discussed some more, and finally realized that this was not the right timing for us to move on. I called my new-found friend back the next day and told him that we simply were not ready to go any further. Thank you but no thanks.

This episode was repeated two more times over the next twenty years. Another job opportunity in Illinois in the 90's and a possibility in Michigan in the mid-2000s. Both were venerable institutions focused on troubled kids looking for experienced leadership. I interviewed for the first position but not the second. Ironically, that last job was the one I really felt I was ready for after more than 30 years at Roundup. I had been a part of a church where the pastor stayed too long, and the separation was not pretty. I didn't want things to work out that way for me, so I actually believed this might be an excellent opportunity at a most appropriate time. Alas, it was not to be.

I included these pieces in my memoir because there were many lessons learned during these times. Sometimes I thought I knew exactly what I wanted and what would be best for all concerned. In the case of Guardian Angel, I realized that my roots had already gotten quite deep in Denver and despite all the good reasons to go, what was most compelling was our need to stay.

For me the evaluation process, what would we lose vs. what would be gained, proved to be crucial. Are we ever able to see things so clearly, so unmistakably, that our choice is easy? On rare occasions perhaps, but what seems right from one perspective, might be disastrous for someone else.

Our bottom line has been to engage in serious discussion and trust in God for discernment during any significant process that affects family, livelihood, and future prospects. Big decisions are never easy by design, so moving ahead with smug assumptions can only cause heartache in retrospect. Life is tough enough without having to kick oneself for years after making an ill-advised or hasty choice. Praise God for His steadying influence as we traverse the often-unsettling seas of life.

CATALONIA RIVIERA MAYA

December 2016

Mexico for the first time: sunshine, palm trees, ocean breezes and a gastronomic extravaganza of mind-boggling proportions.

After a smooth flight, our driver shuttled us expertly down the highway as the sun was setting. Our eyes caught a fleeting glimpse of what was in store for us. Signs along the highway announcing sights and tours virtually shouted at us as we sped to our hotel: "Tulum, Chichen Itza, Xcaret," all exotic adventures awaiting those with the interest and pesos necessary to fulfill their dreams and desires.

Arriving at our destination in the dark only extended our anticipation about the Catalonia resort. A confused hotel clerk dampened our enthusiasm for a moment, but we believed the reservation/cost fiasco would be solved, but obviously not tonight. A late dinner offered momentary respite and a nighttime stroll through the hotel and grounds only whetted our appetites for a daylight tour of the property. Our evening concluded with a first-rate musical of "Aladdin," featuring excellent performances by singers and dancers who made the presentation at a large theater within our hotel. This would be the first of our nightly entertainments which added value to the label of "all inclusive."

Muchachas and Muchachos

Leaning into Life

Tara told us, most excitedly I would add, that we had to get ready for the big foam party on Saturday. She had spoken about this on a number of occasions as we were in the preparatory phase, so no one could quite grasp what she was talking about. True to form, on Saturday afternoon some rather large and interesting equipment was wheeled over to the pool. There were two large barrels along with what looked like a modified cement mixer. Modified indeed! As everyone milled around and in the pool, music began. An announcement followed about "get ready for some foamy fun." And then it started. The cement mixer apparatus was actually a cannon. Lines ran from the barrels into the cannon and we began getting showered with sudsy water all around one end of the pool. A veritable soapy foam shower covered everyone who was brave enough to stay in the pool. This was no short spritz; we were being drenched in soap for what seemed like hours. It was a riot. Certainly, in the annals of swimming pool history, nothing like this had ever happened to any of us before. (The lone exception of course, was Nate and Tara's family who had visited this resort before).

Despite the apparent laid back attitude of our Mexican vacation surroundings, we quickly learned that this place was really go, go, go as in, "go to the buffet, go to the bar, go to the pool, go to the beach." This was a rhythm we quickly learned to master and enjoy. What we also enjoyed each night was exceptional entertainment. This typically began with singers who performed a wide variety of music in the large lounge upstairs, then shows done by many of the poolside activity people along with others in the adjacent large theater. From "Aladdin" and "The Lion King" to Broadway Show Tunes and a Mexican cultural tour complete with authentic singing and dancing, the performers were a talented lot who interacted with the audience both before and after their shows. This made them a real hit with the many kids who were there though it meant late nights for all. Parents, no doubt, hoped for a brief morning respite that resulted from weary children who slept in. Maybe.

"Fat Cat" Catamaran Excursion

Since our hotel was all-inclusive, we were glad that they had so much to offer. However, we did want other experiences, so we booked a snorkeling trip for our full contingent of 18 on a catamaran. Great choice! A smaller craft which offered space for 26 in addition to a skilled crew of five, we launched and cruised the turquoise water for about an hour. The braver souls aboard, mostly our grandchildren, moved forward to the netted prow where they were saturated by both the sun's rays and the surf's spray.

When we reached our snorkeling destination, we listened to our captain's spiel, donned our gear and jumped in. Besides beautiful coral and fish, we saw sting rays, sea turtles, sea urchins, and a small octopus. All too soon we were beckoned back on board as we had a few other surprises left before returning to port.

Back on board we weighed anchor and headed back to sea. The crew typically trolled for whatever might be biting and had two lines in the water as we were slicing our way back to land. After an enjoyable interlude of conversation, a crewman called out that we had a strike. Since each crew member has a job, bringing in our quarry would have to fall on one of the paying customers: our son Nate was quickly selected and the pole was put into his hands. Following the instructions of the crew, he pulled and reeled for some time until he drew the catch of the day up near our vessel. The gorgeous green and yellow

Mahi Mahi had fought hard, breaking the water's surface several times until it was finally subdued and gaffed, a great bit of fun and excitement for all those on board including the ship's crew.

We next headed for a calm inlet where we were encouraged to jump in and swim a bit while one of the mates skillfully and quickly carved the catch into some large fillets. Though Nate had the joy of bringing in the big fellow, the crew had their own system of distributing the catch amongst themselves. They would soon be enjoying a delicious seafood bonanza as part of their day's compensation after the guests left the ship with their photos and memories.

Our next day was reserved for lounging and reciting the many moments of pleasure we had yesterday. One thing that was unique was the daily photographers who traveled the premises, looking for the chance to catch individuals or families at their festive best. Sometimes they brought exotic creatures with them such as cockatoos or parrots or even large lizards. Always they were looking for someone who wanted a little adventure and would be willing to have the animals sit on their head or shoulder. That same evening one could go to a small booth where the day's shots could be viewed and purchased if desired. One more way to make a buck, but a most delightful one for those who took the bait.

The day following, we were ready for our next big adventure, our trip to Tulum. A van pulled up promptly at 8:20 and we were off to meet some others who had made the same choice. We picked up a disgruntled couple who hailed from New Jersey who were certain we wanted to hear about the miseries being inflicted upon them by their hotel. Fortunately, our tribe of five, which included Christina, Levi and Maya, was clear about our own purpose, so we occasionally nodded, but were eager for our van to meet up with our next mode of transport. When we abruptly pulled over to the side of the road after a short ride, we were told that we would soon be greeted by a larger coach that would bring us to our destination. Although unusual by American standards, our meeting on the shoulder of the highway did indeed put us into a comfortable coach that brought us through the forest, stopping in a parking lot where we exited and moved briskly down a path to a cenote'. We took a short refreshing dip in a freshwater pool and headed back to the bus by way of a sandy beach which got our three grandchildren a second chance to get wet. In minutes we were back on the bus headed for our historic destination.

Our guides on the bus gave us some instructions regarding when to meet after our excursion and then parked on the outskirts of the ruins. We were placed into groups by language, English or Spanish, and advised to stay close to our guides at all times. We then began a fairly lengthy walk toward the attraction, observing the area and noting that many others had made the same choice that we had. Upon arrival at the ticket sales area, we were whisked ahead, bypassing the hordes who were standing in line to buy tickets. We were glad that we had signed up in advance and could move forward without the standard hurry up and wait that afflicts so many tours and attractions. Along the way to the actual Tulum site, our pleasant guide gave us lessons in Mayan history and culture before we gained access to the site.

What is noteworthy is the fact that people who we typically consider to be primitive, were actually quite advanced. Many buildings were still standing and appeared to be in remarkably good condition after the passage of more than fifteen centuries. Our house in Denver should do so well. The multitude of lizards who were the current inhabitants didn't seem to mind the press of gawking humanity that came their way in conveyor belt fashion. Tour groups were everywhere and members needed to stay together or they could rapidly find themselves hopelessly lost and wishing they had never left the safety of their resort's pool.

We learned that the Mayans had an intense interest in the skies and the seasons. They closely watched the movement of the sun and its impact as seasons changed. This led them to develop their Mayan calendar and in a unique turn, they were able to combine aspects of their religion, science, and architecture into something most impressive. They built a temple with two windows that were designed to mark both the summer and winter solstices by letting sunlight shine in equally, precisely through those windows on June 21 and December 21. This was a mathematical and cosmological feat of the first order. I shudder to think how many centuries it would take me to figure out what they did, if at all!

After an hour with our guide, we were given time to explore on our own. One could wander among the various buildings, but most folks chose to go down a staircase behind the temple that led to the turquoise sea below. Many got into the water and found an untamed ocean without breakers to slow down the relentless waves that came in and crashed on the shore. After just a few minutes in this wild water, we decided we needed to round up the grandchildren and begin the march back up the steps so we could get our bearings for the trek back to the comfort of our coach.

When we finally got back to our resort, we were ready for a meal and some time by the pool. We realized we were more tired than we thought we'd be, but we all had a healthy respect for the "primitive" people who studied and worked so hard so that we 21st century folks could appreciate them for who they were and what they accomplished.

Our final day found us strolling down to the marina where we saw huge but gentle manatees enjoying a gourmet lettuce buffet administered by their handlers. Performing seals and dolphins leaping out of the water caught our eye, but we especially enjoyed playing catch with a stray dolphin who decided to play with the crowd, tossing a basketball to some and snagging their tosses back to him. It was just a fun, relaxing way to enjoy our final full day in paradise.

This trip will stay with each of us for a very long time. Making memories is what this was all about and I think we accomplished that goal in fine style.

THE SENSUAL AND THE SPIRITUAL

"However, the spiritual is not first, but the natural, and afterward the spiritual." I Cor. 15:46 (NKJV)

Every day I live is fresh and new, whether I am greeted by a cloudless azure sky or a more ominous military gray, replete with low hanging clouds. The air can be as dry as the desert sand causing skin to shrivel or be so laden with moisture that dense fog limits one's visibility and literally brings sweat to the surface. One can often smell a new day, be it pungent or sweet, filled with the stench of burning autumn leaves or the freshness of clean clothes hanging on the backyard clothesline.

I can hear a new day too, whether it be filled with the early roar of work-bound commuters or trucks grinding gears through pre-dawn rush hour traffic. It can also be the early morning quiet of Sunday, the day of rest, broken only by the chirp of a mid-summer cricket who confused his days and nights. I suppose it is even possible to taste a new day through the anticipation of a hearty breakfast or the aftertaste of a late-night dining extravaganza.

What else is there beyond the external sights, sounds, smells, tastes and touches that are universal for all of humanity? Beyond the **sight** of an indescribable sunset, the **sound** of a violin virtuoso, the summertime **smell** of a newly mowed lawn, the exquisite **taste** of a freshly baked peach pie or the **feel** of a perfectly fitting pair of well-made slacks, could there be more?

Indeed. There is an entire inner life that compels even beyond the world of the five senses. The body offers much but the heart, soul, mind and spirit offer more than we can ever think or imagine.

James Vander Kamp

It is fair to say that I have been on a spiritual journey since the day I came into the world. As infants it is unknowing, but already as a child one begins to think about the imponderables of life. As a youngster I don't recall asking my parents any deep questions concerning the meaning of life, but I did wonder about God. If heaven is His home and it is high above the sky, then how can He move so fast to be there when I am scared and really need Him? And how does He do that for everyone who needs Him, since we aren't too good at taking turns in a crisis?

I don't ever recall thinking that I was worthless. I always believed my life had a purpose and that what I did was valuable. That must be because no one told me otherwise. I believe that God created me and everyone else and therefore, life had meaning. Even when I was down I knew that I was not out. In a rational world, things made sense despite many contrary examples. Reading the Bible continues to inspire me and fill me with awe for a God who both loves and punishes; who overlooks my sins because I don't; who is patient yet severe; who is demanding yet merciful; who is firm but kind. As a parent, I was no match for God. I'm sure my children wholeheartedly agree!

Along the way, I have learned some profound lessons. These are things that have sunk deeply into my spirit and guide me through life. Let me put a few before you.

"Look for the miraculous in the ordinary."

"Never forget that your life has a purpose. No matter what age you are, if you haven't found it, keep looking."

"Never limit the kindness you show. You never know

when your simple word or touch will keep someone from going over the edge."

"Ascribe value to every person you meet and always try to be of service to others."

"The difficulty of any undertaking is what gives it meaning."

"Life is never about the adversity we face but rather how we respond to it."

The Bible offers me a treasure-trove of wisdom that defies my ability to follow it, but nonetheless does not stop me from meditating on it or moving into it. Here are just a few:

"He has shown you, O man, what is good; and what does the Lord require of you but to do justly, to love mercy, and to walk humbly with your God." (Micah 6:8)

"Blessed are the merciful, for they shall obtain mercy. Blessed are those who are persecuted for righteousness' sake, for theirs is the kingdom of heaven. You are the salt of the earth. You are the light of the world. Let your light shine before men that they may see your good works and glorify your Father in heaven." (selections from Matt. 5)

"Be strong and of good courage; do not be afraid, nor be dismayed, for the Lord your God is with you wherever you go." (Josh. 1:9)

This small sample is what builds my spirit each day. I always try to remind my 21st century sophisticated self that life is not as complicated as I try to make it. There is certainly evil working in the world but my job is to try to overcome evil with good. It's a lifetime quest but worth the effort.

WORKING OUT

As a boy, running, throwing, catching, jumping, climbing, and wrestling were a natural part of life. Refinement of those activities usually came when one joined a team, whether in the games we orchestrated ourselves as boys or when we were able to join a formal team as we got older. We went from policing ourselves as youngsters to being led by coaches, officials, referees, and umpires.

We didn't realize that there was another angle to our competition: fitness. We weren't in exercise classes to lose weight, improve our balance or develop our agility. We played ball to compete, get better at whatever we were doing, and to have fun. Fat kids could play but they usually didn't do as well because they weren't as fast or coordinated. We never thought about weight loss as an end itself; it usually just happened because one got taller and lost a few pounds in the process of growing up.

I had always loved being active, especially playing sports. Baseball, football, basketball, bowling, tennis and later, skiing were all in my repertoire. I suppose we all know that we won't be able to perform in every category at a high level much beyond late adolescence, but I believed it was well worth trying. For me there was an exhilaration that came with well-coordinated movement coupled with competition. When the demands of team participation were becoming too great, I moved into officiating as a way to stay close to sports and to make a decent side income as well.

By my forties, I could see the handwriting on the wall: a loss a speed, waning agility, and a lifetime of injuries were taking a mighty toll. I could still participate but on a much more limited basis. The dreaded middle-age gut had appeared and I had many responsibilities which kept me from playing. Fortunately, I had a son who was in college and he introduced me to the weight room.

Lifting weights was not something I had ever done or even considered. I saw Charles Atlas in comic book ads when I was younger and saw Jack La Lane do calisthenics on TV; none of it was particularly appealing to me. But when my son called and invited me to join him at the rec center, I figured it was worth a try. So, at 49 I started a new activity that I had never done before: weight lifting.

The first few times I went in I followed Nathan's lead; what did I know about any of this? He was a strapping lad of 21, taller than me and with a fat-free physique. He put me on the bench and told me this would be easier on my back, a safer alternative than bending over and lifting hefty barbells. The problem came when he kept piling on the weights like he had done for himself. I quickly reminded him that I had never done this before and therefore would likely collapse under his oppressive regimen. He backed off the weights and I ended up with 75 pounds as a starting place. With full exertion, I hoisted the bar up several times as directed. The next day I thought the world would end, I was so sore. My body cried out for less, not more. I thought I would never reenter that door, but...

Many years have passed. I still go to the same rec center three days each week. I know people, lots of people. They are nice to me and encourage me as I am entering my dotage. We talk a lot between stations, so we can catch our breath while solving the world's problems. It is a safe place where I have made new friends while gaining a semblance of fitness and tone. I have come to realize that the reason for me to go there remains, but there is so much more to it. Like my men's Bible study, like my writers' club, like other things that I have gone into with a particular purpose in mind, I am moved by so much more. Learning the stories of acquaintances that become friends, hearing heartfelt stories about their joys and sorrows, sharing some intimate details of their lives, all of this in the name of studying, writing, or even, working out.

Who'd a thunk it?

James Vander Kamp

THE TRIP BEYOND BOUNTIFUL

Las Vegas has a multitude of aliases. From "Sin City" to "Lost Wages," the bright lights in the desert are an unlikely place for a major metropolitan area full of contrasts. I was there in April, 2017 for an educational conference titled "Time to Teach." I was attracted to a concept for classroom management which can be used for all grades and all subjects which is designed to reduce stress for teachers and create a better learning environment for students. I loved the concept so I decided to take the plunge and see if this was really for me.

What also drew me to this organization was that they did not talk about wanting teachers only as their representatives. Instead, they stated that they were looking for people with the three Ps: passion, professionalism and personality. Since I have been out of the classroom on a formal basis since 1973, I was hoping that I still might have what it takes to deliver their message to as many teachers as I could.

My arrival at the Golden Nugget, the conference hotel, set me up for an intensive training session over a four-day span. I came alone with a few materials in hand, not knowing how many people would be there, where they were from, or what exactly we would be doing. Each day was very structured, with days beginning at either 7:45 or 8 and sprinting on to 5 or 5:30. Each person had paid for this privilege, including airfare, hotel and most meals (lunch was included). We never saw the light of day during this stretch but stayed on task with training delivered by a series of exceptional presenters, all of whom serve as part of the management team of Time to Teach.

Our topic was classroom management. Times have changed from the days when chewing gum in class or speaking out of turn brought stern reprimands. Now the major concerns often include weapons, drugs, assault, and a bevy of other stress-producing behaviors that are driving teachers out of the classroom. More than 7000 teenagers drop out of school **each day**. Teachers are leaving the profession at an alarming rate as well. Within three years of beginning their careers, fully one-third have left teaching to find another way to make their living. This is more than sobering; it borders on catastrophic.

Having read the book they sent me and having heard the above statistics, I honestly wondered what could be done to save the day. In a very short time I became captivated by their consistent, common sense (and research based) approach to solving these major problems. I became increasingly convinced that the problems described could be handled effectively by the caring people in the classrooms of America provided teachers learned how to solve many of these significant problems by addressing them early in the chain of behaviors, lovingly called, "climbing the staircase to the impossible precipice."

In my professional life, it became increasingly clear that for staff to do their jobs well, they needed to know what the expectations were. This is a universal truth. We expect that students come to school ready, willing, and able to learn. That is increasingly **not** the case. Teachers need to restate all the obvious things to assure themselves that their expectations are clear to their students. Intervening early in the cycle of misbehavior produces amazing results for schools that are trapped in the unending cycle of minor misbehavior, ascending the ladder to a point of no return. Schools that reported sending hundreds of students to the office have seen those numbers drop by 90% or more in just one year after having been trained and implementing this system. Who wouldn't want to be the Rock

Star who delivered this message to teachers whose careers were on the rocks?

Beyond the training day there was a little time left for some night life. The Golden Nugget is on Fremont Street and is part of what is known as "The Fremont Experience." Experience indeed. In addition to the plethora of slot machines and smoke-filled rooms, there was an overhead experience that was mind-boggling. They had created a light show canopy that extended for blocks as one walked down the memorable lane. Music blaring, lights flashing, zip liners careening through the air; enough to give the good Dr. Mesmer a headache.

I am not sure why they wanted the hordes to look up so much because there certainly was plenty to keep one's interest at ground level. Lights flashing from every building, concert stages providing unending, ear-splitting sound, ubiquitous advertising for the next buffet at a bargain price if you cared to eat your steak and lobster before 5 p.m., all vied for attention. Then there were the shirtless, well-muscled men seeking ladies to join them for photographs. Many women whose own proportions did not match their suitors signed up and certainly became celebrities to friends and family from afar.

Last, and certainly not the least, were the women. It was amazing to see how many young and even some not so young women forgot to bring their clothing. Street corner exposure was at a maximum and modesty at a minimum. It made me wonder about what had happened to them in their family lives during their growing up years. A bad school experience? Poor parenting? A loss of moral compass? Overabundant self-confidence? What would drive someone to stand naked before all the world to be leered at and photographed with strangers whose interest focused on their curvaceous figures alone without regard for the circumstances that had brought these women to this point? Since I spoke to no one on this subject, it will have to remain a mystery until I can gather the courage to ask. Maybe next time.

My conference experience was inspiring. I came away with a new-found zest for sharing what I had learned and will now need to cultivate an entrepreneurial spirit that at best lies dormant deep within me. I will be selling myself: my passion, my professionalism, and my personality. Presentation is really King when it comes to winning over an audience, be it adult educators or youthful students. My challenge lies before me.

THE NEXT GENERATION

In covering my life, I have made several mentions about some very significant people without providing much in the way of detail. That changes right here, right now. The significant people in question happen to be our grandchildren who, thus far, have gotten barely a nod in this memoir.

Katie's first-born, Christina, came on the scene long before any of her successors. Friday, October 9, 1998 was the 25th anniversary of Roundup Fellowship and we were celebrating at a hotel with friends and supporters of our organization. Katie, nine months pregnant, sat at our table in a most uncomfortable state. As Executive Director, I was preoccupied throughout the evening and couldn't really pay much attention to her. She went home with Elaine and I stayed to wrap a few things up after good-byes were said and the guests had left. I was bushed, and when I got home around midnight, I noted that all were tucked into bed, so I decided to follow suit.

For some reason, there were a few early birds up the next morning, so I felt obligated to join them. A quick check found the cupboard to be bare, so I decided to make a short trek to King Soopers for Saturday morning essentials, cereal and milk. At seven a.m. one can move quite smartly through a grocery store, so I was headed back in no time to assuage the hunger of the early risers.

As I came up our street I immediately noted an ambulance conspicuously parked in front of our house. Since we have many elderly neighbors, I wondered if someone had suffered a heart attack or some other emergency. Before I got to the first step of our walkway, the front door flew open and daughters Missy and Andrea lurched frantically forward. "Dad,

Katie had her baby!" Those words moved me into hyper-speed, and as I entered the door, the flurry of movement and words became a blur. Katie and her new child were already in the ambulance and were being whisked off to the hospital as Elaine conveyed the bizarre tale of the arrival of our first grandchild, with her participating as mid-wife. When Job heard the tale of woe about his family and fortune in rapid succession he proclaimed, "That which I have feared most has come upon me!" Elaine could easily have made the same remarks but for a decidedly different reason. Delivering our first grandchild was never in her plans.

With such an auspicious beginning to life, Christina immediately had a special place in my heart. Since she and Katie would live with us for almost five years, until Katie married Luke, we developed a relationship that I have never had with any other grandchild. It was like having our first child all over again with feeding, changing, holding, playing, reading and all the other elements that go with a neonate in the developmental process. Katie worked at a day care center, so she could take Christina with her every day, but every night they came home and we were able to see our first grandchild every day of her life during those early years.

There were many wonderful moments during that time, but I must convey what stayed with me the most. Christina was exposed to Christian influences from her earliest days, so singing songs and going to church were common practices for her. She learned the song, "The B-I-B-L-E, yes that's the book for me," at an early age. When she would see me reading the Bible, she would often come over and say, "Read the B-I-B-L-E to me, Papa." Obviously, not every passage is suited to the understanding of a two to three-year-old, so I had to do some improvising. The Old Testament story of Joseph and his attempted seduction by Potiphar's wife took some clever retelling if I do say so.

As the years passed we noticed that Christina showed a penchant for reading, writing and for horses. The latter came because of connections we made with other families during her homeschool years of 5th – 8th grades. She joined 4H and rode regularly and performed quite well, earning numerous ribbons along the way. She also got to do the uninspiring job of "mucking" stalls as part of her board for the horse she rode. All of this helped her realize that life was not a free ride and eventually helped her win a ribbon as Reserve Grand Champion at the Colorado State Fair in Pueblo in her last year in 4H.

After moving to Greeley for high school, we got an unexpected surprise of having her entire family join us again in our home in Denver due to some financial setbacks they suffered during her junior year. They lived with us during her senior year where she had the difficult task of transferring to a new school for her final year of high school. We were very proud of her ability to fit in, make friends, and to perform at a high level. Graduation was a proud moment for the entire family.

Currently, she is a freshman at Arapahoe Community College and the family is still with us. This gets us in on a lot of things that we would never know about, but it also allows me the privilege of helping her with some of her writing assignments. She is very disciplined and responsible, so I am more of a "talk it through buddy" rather than a heavy-handed overseer in the homework department. She needs little direction but my being available has strengthened our relationship. I cannot imagine having similar access to any other grandchild's life, so I am thankful for the twists and turns that Providence used to bring us closer together.

Her brother, Levi, six years her junior, is our second grandchild. Now a 7th grader at Hamilton Middle School, he too has had an interesting Odyssey. When his family lived near us in Denver, he became quite interested in the fact that his sister was being homeschooled by Grandma. When the appointed time for school came, Levi called requesting admission to Grandma's Basement School. Since his sister was already a student, it was difficult to deny him admission, so the student body doubled in one fell swoop in 2011. He remained a student until they moved to Greeley.

Levi is his own man. He has never seen a ball he did not like, regardless of shape. He has played soccer, baseball, football, and basketball. While some may begin thinking of career options as they move toward high school, I'm sure he already has his picked: professional basketball. On occasion he needs reminding that there is an academic component to life as well. When he focuses, he can do a fine job in the classroom. He does, however, require some prodding occasionally in order to bring that to fruition.

Levi is a very tender soul. He shows love easily and is well-loved by his cousins and other family members. He understands that God has a special place for him and he reciprocates back to God. He is bright, fun-loving, and eager to try new things, particularly if they involve any kind of competition. It is still early in the game for him, but we are excited to see what God has in store for him as he wends his way through life. Right now, I would say his three favorite statements are, "I know;" "I don't know;" and "You're crazy, Papa." We do expect some verbal expansion as the years go by.

Our son Nathan and his sweet wife Tara have three

children, all of whom we gladly claim as ours too. Maya Elaine, with her grandma's name following hers, is fast approaching her 12th birthday. She takes after her Dad with a talent for drawing, but she has enough of me in her as well to have already shown herself an able thespian with a sweet singing voice. She has always had a quirky side to her but that has only made her more endearing as the years have passed. As a small child she had some significant health problems which resulted in abdominal surgeries, but she has recovered very nicely and is now strong in both mind and body.

Although friendly and social, she also demonstrates a solitary bent. Even in a crowd, she can go off by herself and begin collecting whatever strikes her fancy, from rocks to shells to bugs. I suspect this side of her may someday express itself in writing. She is a cheerful child who smiles often and is quick to hug, even after long absences from us. As any proud parent or grandparent would say, we expect great things from her someday.

Tyler James, with my name in second place, is nine. He carries the weight of maintaining the Vander Kamp name into the future as he is the only male descendant who can bear the family surname. A cheerful, energetic lad, Tyler has interests that include hip hop dance, drama and, you may have guessed, sports. His dad has coached him most of the time but this year he branched out into a basketball league with someone else at the helm. Like his cousin Levi, Tyler is constantly on the move. Emotions run high with him and we think that will be a place he will need to learn some control as he progresses through life.

Like so many boys we have seen (including his dad), we have noted that an elevated body temperature must be endemic. It is hard for him to keep his shirt on for very long as he runs, jumps, falls, and slides around the yard. A boy's internal thermostat must be set rather low because it doesn't take much for him to toss his shirt aside as he bounds on to whatever next activity presents itself. The upside may be that he will need a smaller wardrobe than some, particularly shirts!

Nora Grace Snizek, Todd and Missy's first born, is a doll. She is a spitting image of her mother without the spit. Now eight, she has endless interests that have drawn out her budding natural abilities. Father Todd, a hockey enthusiast, had her on skates at an early age. She takes lessons on the ice and we have seen her perform at the Broadmoor Arena in Colorado Springs. She is a quick learner and is always willing to try new stunts as she glides across the surface and twirls to complete her session. We think some of this comes from her obsession with doing cartwheels, which can happen at any time and in any place.

Nora also has some inherited gifts in the realm of art. She draws amazingly well and loves to create pictures and paintings. We know there is a gene somewhere in there because her mother and uncle are very talented in this area as well. The best thing is that she enjoys it, and nothing beats exuberance. Academics suit her as well, so we may have a Renaissance Woman on our hands as she advances through life. Her sweet, inquisitive personality is an asset to her and will be no matter what she chooses to do in the future.

Her charming sister, Lucy Mae, is six. She is a complex mix of smiles and tears, concern and competitiveness, sociability, and independence. She plays well with others but can comfortably entertain herself for long periods of time without the need of interactive reinforcement. I believe that the ability to engage in solitary play speaks well for imagination and creativity. She is a child that one can just enjoy due to her winsome personality.

Since she is on the front end of her educational journey in kindergarten, it is hard to make too many long-range career predictions. She has made some memorable statements, though, regarding her view of pre-school. "All we do is work, work, work." I was worn out just hearing her. She is loving and will always jump into a lap for a hug and some cuddling. I'll take that any day before she's ready to enter that PhD. program.

Grandchild number seven in our quiver is little Annie Vander Kamp. She was the child of much discussion, coming five years after her brother Ty. Since Nate and Tara already had a girl and boy, they thought they had the complete family. We are forever grateful that their love for children sought a further extension. Annie is a delightful child who loves singing and reading books. There truly is no end to the book reading as she is content to hear the same story read to her multiple times. She is a fan of the Berenstain Bears and, fortunately, there are many books to choose from. At age three we know her only from our brief visits over her short lifespan.

What we do know, however, is good. She is a great companion for her devoted mother and a willing accomplice for her two older siblings. She is more timid at this stage but has a pair of role models who will, no doubt, lead her into plenty of mischief. Initially, she was understandably stand-offish toward us, visitors who acted like we knew her when she was still trying to figure out who we were. Thankfully, her fear has subsided and she is ready to be held and carried and loved like everyone else. We look forward to building our relationship with her over many years to come.

The last grandchild to come on the scene as of this writing is two-year old Vance, better known as "Vancy" to his family. Like Tyler for the Vander Kamps, so too Vance for the Snizeks, carries the weighty responsibility of perpetuating the family name. A cheerful, playful tyke, Vance is an engaging little man who loves to be held and carried when he's not running around. He has a cheerful disposition and is a willing napper and sleeper, things that are always highly prized by parents and grandparents alike.

One thing that we have all noticed about him is his sense of humor. Even with limited language, Vance can draw us in with his charming statements and twinkling eyes. If a sense of humor is closely correlated to intelligence, then we have a budding Einstein on our hands. Two years are a short sample but somehow we are sure that this boy will make his mark on the world. I love that boy.

James Vander Kamp

LIFE, RISING

(I wrote this for Christina after reading from a few literary
friends, Walt Whitman, William Shakespeare and Langston
Hughes. I thank them for some inspiration, but the verse is
mine alone).

High School graduation…

The world is before you,
You are free to go wherever you choose.
From humble beginnings,
Now all the world is your stage,
Be it for soliloquy, duet, or chorus.

There are many parts to play,
For you, so far, they have been
Infant,

Leaning into Life

Child,
Youth.
But what is that peeking above the horizon?
Could it be Adult,
Ready to assume your new estate,
Having crossed the graduate's requisite rite of passage?

Ah, but what else?

Your passage is less secure now,
The markers are murkier
And the people are quirkier.
What you will find is less predictable
And may even prove despicable.

James Vander Kamp

Do you know yet what you want,
Where you will go
Or with whom you will travel?
Is your character strong enough
So that you will know
When things start to unravel?

None of us is fully formed
At any age so
Keep the trust,
Have dreams and
Hold on to them.
Remember:
They are yours and no one else's,
So you will know when it's your time
To fly.

CHANGING OF THE GUARD

As the patriarch of my now multi-generational family, I recall with great satisfaction and fondness the many hiking trips we made and continue to make to the mountains. I always looked forward to taking our children on forays into the wilderness, pointing out the finer points of flora and fauna as we trekked to some waterfall or mountain meadow where we could enjoy a bucolic picnic seated on a fallen tree and enjoying the vista laid before us.

As our youngsters aged, I still made it my end to remain at the head of the line. As the saying goes, "if you're not the lead dog, the scenery never changes." I wanted to be the first to point out whatever appeared before us, offering whatever erudite explanation I could for the phenomenon. I suppose this was a matter of pride on my part, but over time I grudgingly let one of our then-teenagers assume the lead and make the initial discovery, whatever it was. Secretly, I knew I could assume the helm at any time and lead the charge to points unknown.

Then along came the next generation. Grandchildren needed to know who was in charge and how these types of expeditions needed to operate. It took a steady hand and a strong voice to keep the urchins in line so that everyone would toe the mark and know that Papa was still the captain of the journey. Despite a slowing pace and an occasional need for trekking poles, there was no doubt in my mind that I was still he who gave the marching orders.

Recently, however, I have noticed that either my pace was slowing at an alarming rate, or my grandchildren had quickened theirs markedly. When five-year-old Lucy looked back on a recent hike in Vail and asked, "Are you okay, Papa?", my mind went into a brief turmoil. Could it be that age, coupled with injury, had done me in? Was I no longer qualified to consistently be the leader of the pack?

The moment of truth came recently on an arduous hike above Breckenridge to a lovely spot, Continental Falls. It was roughly three miles to our destination and I was in charge of my eldest pair of grandchildren: Christina, 18 and her younger brother Levi, 12. As we began our walk, it became obvious that I was no longer a match for this dynamic duo. In short order, I began trailing them and noted that the distance between us was increasing with virtually every step. Occasionally, they would stop for a brief water break, during which time I would arrive at their resting spot, only to have to continue moving because their rest period had already ended. So much for Papa getting refreshment.

What have I learned from this recent adventure? That I can still hike, albeit more slowly. That my joy in serving as the Lead Dog must give way to the robust generation that is removed from me by a factor of two. That my new-found joy can now show itself in my sense of wonder at how those kids move so far, so fast without any seeming loss of energy. This baton passed without a manual exchange but instead with the silent but happy thought that I am still included.

James Vander Kamp

THE ROADMAP OF MY LIFE

As I look into the mirror now,
What do I see?
A wrinkle, a crease,
a crinkle, a beast?
It was not always so.
I was young once with
few responsibilities
and no bills to pay.
I faced few hardships
and encountered minimal setbacks.
But things change.
What can I say?

My face is the roadmap of my life:
the surprises I had enlarged my eyes
while the grudges I carried narrowed them.

Leaning into Life

Sorrows added "crow's feet" around them
and my forehead added creases
when my children got sick
or learned to drive,
started to date and
went out on their own.
A deeper line was added when my Dad died.

But when I look again, I notice that
my laugh lines have grown the most.
From childhood jokes
to high school pranks,
to the joy of friendship,
to the greatest joy of
love…love…love.
The joy of seeing children born,
children marry,
grandchildren born,
and grandchildren growing up.
Joy…joy…joy.

I guess I really don't mind getting older,
if that is what it means.
After all, my face reminds me
that the route I've followed is
most pronounced along
the laugh lines.
Joy has ruled the day and my life
More than sorrow and grudges or fears
which are too few to mention.
I don't mind looking into the mirror
because the road map is easy to follow:
Love, joy, laughter…

James Vander Kamp

I'm grateful for the life I've lived.

Rhythms

Life is full of natural rhythms. In the summer, despite heat, drought, thunder, lightning, even hail and tornadoes, we know that the moderating influence of autumn is not far behind with cooler temperatures and a less volatile atmosphere. Each day has its own rhythm as well as we cheer a sunrise, move energetically into the day, only to find our energy waning as the day progresses and nightfall comes. These are simple everyday occurrences that we take for granted because they repeat themselves thousands of times in our lifetimes.

But now I find I am in uncharted territory. It is a region I have wondered about, read about, and talked about, but have yet to experience. I am referring, of course, to old age. I know that I'm not there yet – do you think? I've moved through other life stages and typically looked forward to each: childhood to adolescence, adolescence to adulthood, even moving into middle age did not overwhelm me. In fact, I am thankful to marketing masterminds of demography who continue to give us hope by expanding categories to include things like "middle age" and "late middle age," or even telling us that "60 is the new 40" or reminding us that "you are as old as you think." Hmmm.

Here I am, almost 70. I have yet to figure out the rhythm for this stage. I still have vigor but I don't feel particularly vigorous; I have energy but am not always so energetic. I like to hike but I prefer flat ground over hills, level surfaces over bumpy, and trekking poles for stability over simply swinging my arms as I saunter along. I lift weights but I find myself looking for someone to talk to between stations instead of simply resting briefly. I mow the lawn but I rest between doing the front and the back. Maybe these things are part of the new rhythm. Hmmm.

No doubt there are many keys to this stage that I haven't found yet. Not that the way is blocked or locked, but maybe I'm just not ready to embrace what I see. After all, **old people** are limited: they don't like to drive at night, so they don't go out as much as they did before. They are less sure of themselves in a variety of situations, especially unfamiliar ones, so they don't try as many new things as before. They go to bed earlier, so they eat earlier. They often take lots of pills to regulate their bodies because their bodies no longer cooperate the way they once did. All of this is of concern, especially if I have not identified with the new rhythm of being an old person.

That's it! Maybe I don't identify because I'm not old! After all, I really am in "late middle age," not "old age." I still don't wear reading glasses. I'm okay with driving at night. I still enjoy new experiences. Okay, I grudgingly accept hiking with trekking poles because my lifetime of sports participation has left me with more than a few injuries, aches and pains. I never go to bed before 10:30 and I know when to stop taking in liquids during the evening so I can extend my sleep time. So what if I mow the lawn in increments; that's what retirement allows me to do.

I am trying to be responsible as I **approach** old age. We bought a funeral plan. We have a will and an estate plan. We updated our life insurance and have long term care insurance. Surely, these are all signs of responsible adulthood, not signs of becoming dotards. Yes, it is clear to me: I have not yet entered that last stage so let's keep the rhythm we have going strong!

Greenwich Lullaby

(I wrote this while a junior in high school
in 1966. The original title was simply **Time**,
but it received the new title at the suggestion
of my English teacher, Bob Hoekstra).

What is time?
Time is the

> ever-moving,
> never changing,
> incessant prodder of rearranging,
> forward staring,
> backward glaring,
> never caring in its daring.

What is time?
Time is the

> Controller of men,
> Recorder for the world,
> Possessor of ills,
> Professor of good,
> Dial for the world.

What is time?
Time is the

> never moving,
> ever-changing,
> deceased prodder of rearranging,
> forward glaring,
> backward staring,
> always caring in its daring.

What is time?

James Vander Kamp

Time is the
          Traverse of men,
          Decoder for the world,
          Possessor of good,
          Professor of ills,
          Dial for the world.

ADAGES TO LIVE BY

As the years pass, we all accumulate some "wisdom of the ages." From our earliest remembrance, to yesterday's conversation, things draw our attention and go into our memory bank. These can range from snippets to extended passages but they are things that resonate with us that we hope we can retrieve at the right time. There are numerous books written that contain famous quotes by famous people, but how about thoughts from the less-than famous? This is my chance to offer a few.

I can honestly say some of these come from some of those famous people. There will be no attribution to anyone other than me however because, quite honestly, I'm not sure I would give credit to the right person. Therefore, take them for what they are: a random list of thoughts, proverbs, and, I hope, common sense observations about life. I hope that something in here will resonate and bless you.

"The problem with life is it's so daily."

"I try to take one day at a time, but sometimes several attack me all at once."

"Your attitude will determine your altitude."

"There are two ways to be fooled. One is to believe what isn't true; the other is to refuse to believe what is true."

"The difficulty of any undertaking is what gives it meaning."

"During the course of my life there have been times when I had delusions of adequacy."

"After a forty-year career, I noticed that I had become

an overnight success."

"Life is never about the adversity we face but rather, how we respond to it."

"Look for the miraculous in the ordinary."

"Being a perfectionist can get you in trouble. Sometimes it's okay to say, 'good enough' even when you know it isn't."

"There's a reason the windshield is bigger than the rearview mirror. What is before you matters more than what is in the past."

"When I was young, the days seemed endless. Now the years seem to fly by."

"Be observant. You can learn a lot by paying attention."

"Consciousness is that disorienting period between naps."

"Never be so open-minded that you let your brains leak out."

"Never be too preoccupied with making a living that you forget to make a life."

"Always be of service to others."

"Never forget that your life has a purpose. No matter what age you are, if you haven't found it, keep looking."

"We are often reminded that life is a marathon, not a sprint. Actually, take it as a pilgrimage, with a pleasing death capping off a satisfying life. In that way, we can all arrive at the same destination while charting our own personal course. Always remember that though detours may abound, God will be next to you the entire way."

"Communicating with God is the most extraordinary experience imaginable, yet at the same time it's the most natural one of all. God is present in us at all times, our divine link to Him. He is omniscient and omnipotent, yet personal and loves us without conditions."

"Never limit the kindness you show. You never know when your simple word or touch will keep someone from going over the edge."

"Don't be an imposter. It is okay to be the real you."

"You don't need to live austerely but you should be able to keep your necessities in life from expanding to the absurd."

"Life is daunting enough without having a thin skin about it. Buck up and dump the self-pity."

"At any stage of life, put your affairs in order. If you always think you have until tomorrow, you may be unpleasantly surprised when you don't."

"Marry well and be a full contributor to your marriage. Your vows should be solemn but bring your sense of humor to the party."

"It's okay to be a little eccentric; just don't make it your calling card."

"Work hard, play hard. Plan accordingly."

James Vander Kamp

"Die young, as late as possible."

"If everything seems to be under control, maybe you aren't going fast enough."

"Remember that each day has enough trouble of its own. There's no need to burden today with what you don't know about tomorrow."

"Mark your trail. Build monuments large and small. Remember good times and bad. Limit your laments and savor your joys."

"Never forget: you will have to live with the choices you make. Do your best to make good ones."

"Failure is an experience, not a person."

"No one is guaranteed the successes they covet, no matter how much or who they sacrifice in the name of the success they crave."

"Long term success is most influenced by your authenticity, your expertise, and your enthusiasm."

"Strive not so much to succeed but to do the right thing."

"In your working life always think of yourself as a company of one. That should always assure maximum effort toward a goal of excellent performance no matter who you work for."

"You should always be more gracious and more grateful. Take advantage of your opportunities to do both."

"Gratitude is not only the greatest of virtues, but the

parent of all others."

"There are plenty of shallow, pedantic people who are a mile wide and an inch deep. Strive for depth over breadth."

"Resolve always trumps any resolution you make. Become more resolute in every endeavor in which you are engaged."

"After many years of working out, I have come to believe that I have the body of a god – Buddha."

"As I look at society today, I often cringe. Someday, when the autopsy of history is completed, I believe that they will find that the cause of death is suicide."

"It is commonly thought that the protected and easy life is the best way to live. Yet the lives of the noblest and strongest among us prove exactly the opposite. It is the endurance of hardship and perseverance through adversity that makes a person. It is that factor which distinguishes between merely existing or living a vigorous life. It is hardship which builds our character."

James Vander Kamp

BUT WHAT OF TOMORROW?

Today I say, "I love you"
But can I also speak to the past
When I say "I have loved you"?

Yes, most emphatically.

But what of the future?
Can I declare my love for
Days not yet lived,
For heights of joy not yet experienced,
For depths of sorrow not yet known,
For times of adulation inexplicable
Or desperation unpredictable?

Without turning a calendar's page
Can I be certain that the vicissitudes of life
Will not modify my heart

Leaning into Life

Nor plunge my soul
Into its darkest night
So that I cannot vouch for the love
That I so easily expressed
A day, a month, a year, a decade or more ago?

Again, I say yes, most emphatically.

For our love is not based on
Circumstance
But on law.
I intend to be a law keeper
Not a law breaker,
To fulfill my promise made long ago
To never leave you or forsake you.

You remain now and forever, the Apple of my eye.

I love you.

> To Elaine,
> Valentine's Day, 2016

James Vander Kamp

Address to Timothy Christian High School Graduation, 2011

Thank you very much for this great honor. I know that my allotted time is short, so I will be basing my talk tonight on the principle of the 3 B's: be interesting, be brief, and be seated.

With that as my prolegomena, let's begin.

I had the privilege of attending Timothy for all twelve years of my education. For the first eight, I walked to school, sometimes with siblings, sometimes with friends. I don't want to romanticize those years, or the high school years that followed, but I have often thought about how valuable my Christian education was. I never paid a dime toward my tuition, yet I know what sacrifices my parents - and your parents - had to make to send me here and you as well.

The wonderful thing is that that tradition continues today and all of you are beneficiaries of families who cared enough so that you could participate in the excellent, Christ-centered educational program that Timothy still is today. There remains an exceptional base of support that keeps this place alive and I for one salute all you parents, grandparents and friends of Timothy who continue to make the sacrifices necessary to keep quality Christian education available to all those who desire it.

For you graduates, I have a few words specifically for you. I started with the three B's and I would like to conclude with the four P's.

The first is that you need to be **passionate**. Find something that draws you in and hang onto it. I have worked for my employer, Roundup Fellowship, for 37 years and I still find my work compelling. Your time at Timothy may have exposed you to something that calls to you. Heed that call and maintain that emotion; it will carry you through the times when you might want to second guess yourself, and believe me, you will second guess yourself.

Second, be **positive**. Believe in yourself and believe in others. Let hope mobilize you. The God of all hope created you for a purpose and if you pursue that purpose with a positive attitude you will be amazed what you can accomplish.

Third, be **prepared**. This is not just the Boy Scouts' motto, but it is for everyone. There is no substitute for preparation. In your years of test-taking, you know when you have studied enough to do your best. Life is all about preparation. Any coach will tell you that the team that prepares well will perform well. You are on the cusp of great things and you have attended a school that has offered you exceptional preparation for your next steps. Take full advantage by making preparation a priority in your life. Relentlessly prepare.

Finally, be **persevering**. Romans 5 reminds us that "tribulation produces perseverance and perseverance, character." An achiever is one who has been tried and endured. That is the essence of character. Let your character define you. Be known as a person who will see things through, even when the obstacles seem to be overwhelming. Be persevering.

Keep the four P's in your arsenal and God will use you mightily.

Thank you for this wonderful opportunity to share this special occasion with all of you.

Here I am, flanked by my brother Dick and sister Pat, holding the plaque I received for being chosen "Distinguished Alumnus of 2011." We are all graduates of Timothy Christian, along with my brother John who did not make this picture.

Leaning into Life

James Vander Kamp

ACKNOWLEDGEMENT BY THE AUTHOR

A memoir isn't an autobiography that tries to tell the whole story, but it should give readers a true taste of what my life is all about, letting them "lean in" to the stories I have shared in this manuscript. I am thankful that I grew up in a more innocent, straightforward era. We faced the same issues that every generation must face, but could approach them in a less complicated fashion. The "fifty shades of gray" that add layers to living and make life so perplexing were not present in my formative years. Certainly changes came as I moved through life, but by then my foundation had been firmly established, giving me a leg up as I confronted the big questions of life.

The shining light has always been family who shined that light on the God of our fathers and His Son Jesus Christ. As I ponder the future of our own children and grandchildren, I hope we will be able to remember and discuss some of the things I have recorded here. After all, this memoir is about all of us and the legacy that I hope will be shared with future generations of the Vander Kamp clan.

I would be remiss if I did not highlight the contribution made by my granddaughter Christina Shires and her good friend Emma Pond. The technical pieces of formatting, inserting pictures, and so much more, finally allowed this work to come to fruition. My fearful and clueless approach led to great frustration, but these two young ladies bailed me out and brought this manuscript to its effervescent conclusion. They have my lifelong gratitude for saving me from myself.

36208779R00095

Made in the USA
San Bernardino, CA
18 May 2019